THE EXPE
OF WOME
SECOND WORLD WAR

War
Stories

DAVID BOLTON

The History Press

Front cover image: Mrs Clark and her child emerge from their Anderson shelter unhurt after the destruction of their house during the bombing raid on Filton, north Bristol, on 25 September 1940. (© David Facey. Facey Collection. Bristol Archives: 41969/1/80)

First published 2022

The History Press
97 St George's Place, Cheltenham,
Gloucestershire, GL50 3QB
www.thehistorypress.co.uk

ISBN 978 0 7509 9956 4

Typesetting and origination by The History Press
Printed and bound in Great Britain by TJ Books Limited, Padstow, Cornwall.

Trees for Life

Contents

Introduction

This book all started with a conversation I had with my mother-in-law, Mary Fox. She told me how she married in haste — in her lunch hour, in fact — very soon after war was declared. Mary's newly acquired husband, George, a young army officer, was subsequently sent off to fight the Japanese in Burma. When he left, neither of them knew that she was pregnant. Mary, now effectively a single mother, had to find somewhere, anywhere, to live.

Her pillar-to-post life in temporary accommodation continued for the next four years. She also had to earn a living of sorts.

Finally, sometime after VJ Day, Major George Fox met his daughter for the very first time. Husband and wife were almost strangers; father and daughter were complete strangers. The army then decided that it was perfectly reasonable to send a man who'd been away fighting for years to work at the Nuremberg trials in Germany. The war, for my mother-in-law, was not an easy time.

Those were the bare bones of her story. Sadly, she died two weeks after our conversation so the full story of her experiences as an ordinary woman living through extraordinary times will never be told. But her death made me think that there must be thousands of women with similar stories and unless somebody recorded them quickly, they would be lost forever. I set about contacting as many women as possible of a certain age and, before long, one contact led to another and then another.

The women I spoke to came from a variety of social backgrounds. One was used to having servants do more or less everything for her and the declaration of war unfortunately put paid to her plans to go 'orff' to a finishing school in Paris; another was the daughter of a docker, who had to make do with candles rather than electric lights, an outside toilet and one bath a week in a tin tub in the kitchen.

The result is, I believe, an honest and accurate retelling of their stories – the war stories of over sixty women. The pity of it is that most of them have since died.

Along with these interviews I have also included numerous entries from the wartime diaries of three women and excerpts from the unpublished memoirs of two others. All contain an endlessly fascinating mixture of the momentous and the entirely domestic and trivial.

This book is not intended to be a formal history of the roles that women played in the Second World War. It is, instead, a collection of unique first-hand stories and accounts, some of them quirky and bordering on the confessional, but all of them honest and revealing. Together, they amount to a fascinating history of what a varied cross-section of women experienced, felt and achieved during those historic years.

George Fox who was sent off to fight in Burma for over three years.

Mary Fox, the author's mother-in-law, who was the original inspiration for this book.

Acknowledgements

I'd like to thank all those who helped me in the writing of this book:

Chris Bray, who first put me in touch with his mother, Hazel Bray, and has helped enormously with the photographs in this book.

Gilly Bray who also helped with the photographs and allowed me to use the diaries of her mother, Joan Hancox (née Williams).

Cameron Kennedy, for putting me in touch with many of the women I interviewed.

Audrey Swindells, whose memoirs appear in the book.

Steve Stunt, for helping me with the photographs and telling me about the experiences of his mother, Irene Stunt.

Rob Swindells, for reading and commenting positively on the manuscript.

Sue Brierly-Fellows, for allowing me to use the memoirs of her mother, Lorna Green.

Bruce Fellows, for reading the manuscript and commenting on it constructively.

Sue Stopps, for being so encouraging about the whole project.

Christopher Martin, for reading the original manuscript and coming up with stern but wise criticisms which helped me to improve it considerably.

Many other people, who shall remain nameless, who helped by lending me photographs of their mothers to accompany several of the stories in this book.

Hilary Bolton, my wife, for checking the manuscript for glaring errors and making suggestions on what could be omitted.

My children, for tolerating my retelling of the stories in this book — many times.

The Monday Club, for listening to my frequent and tedious references to its progress, or lack of progress.

Jonathon Hyams, for helping me with all things technological.

Amy Rigg at The History Press, for first accepting the book for publication and then giving invaluable advice about its extent and content.

Alex Boulton, for being such a tolerant and helpful editor.

And finally, to the many women I interviewed, and their families, who were prepared to answer my interminable questions, donate photographs and tell me about their experiences in the war. Without them, the book would not have been possible.

The Prime Minister, Neville Chamberlain, declaring war on Germany on 3 September 1939. (Pictorial Press Ltd/Alamy Stock Photo)

1

In the Beginning

At 10 a.m. on Sunday, 3 September 1939, the BBC told its listeners to stand by for an announcement of 'national importance'. Every fifteen minutes thereafter, listeners were told that the Prime Minister would make an announcement at 11.15 a.m. Music and a talk on 'How to make the most of tinned foods' were broadcast in between.

Finally, an announcer declared, 'This is London. You will now hear a statement from the Prime Minister.' After a pause, Neville Chamberlain intoned in a flat, doom-laden voice:

I am speaking to you from the Cabinet Room of 10 Downing Street. This morning, the British ambassador in Berlin handed the German Government a final note stating that unless we heard from them by 11 o'clock that they were prepared at once to withdraw their troops from Poland, a state of war would exist between us. I have to tell you now that no such undertaking has been received and that consequently, this country is at war with Germany.

His speech concluded:

Now, may God bless you all and may he defend the right. For it is evil things that we shall be fighting against, brute force, bad faith, injustice, oppression and persecution. And against them I am certain that right will prevail.

Winston Churchill, who was appointed First Lord of the Admiralty that same day, pronounced with a typically orotund flourish in the Commons the next day:

> This is not a question of fighting for Danzig or fighting for Poland. We are fighting to save the whole world from the pestilence of Nazi tyranny and in defence of all that is most sacred to man.

Now, for both men, the gloves were off. No need for the diplomatic niceties like 'Herr Hitler', which they had used before – they were now free to unequivocally condemn a malevolent dictator.

After this broadcast, a series of short, official announcements were made. These included a prohibition on the blowing of whistles and the blaring of horns as they might be confused with air-raid warnings.

Minutes after the declaration of war, huge numbers of people stood outside their front doors looking up at the cloudless blue sky, expecting German bombers to appear overhead at any moment. Others stayed inside and filled baths and basins with water to tackle the expected incendiary bombs, while some hastily nailed blankets over their windows in preparation for the expected gas attack.

Then, at 11.50 a.m., an air-raid warning sounded in London, followed soon after by the 'All Clear'. It was later disclosed that an over-eager spotter had seen a plane in the sky just off the south coast at 11.30 a.m. and assumed, wrongly, that it was an incoming German bomber. In fact, it was a French transport plane en route to London. One unnamed person died of heart failure as a result of this false alarm, the very first person to die in the war.

It was also on the very first day of the war that the RAF 'bombed' Germany, although there was no TNT involved, only paper. A total of 6 million propaganda leaflets were dropped, weighing a total of 13 tons. Among many claims made in the leaflet was the 'fact' that 'The German people do not have the means to sustain protracted warfare. You are on the verge of bankruptcy!' The leaflets reportedly kept the German civilian population well stocked in toilet paper for many months.

It would be totally wrong, however, to think that the declaration of war came out of the blue. In fact, the lead-up to hostilities was protracted, uncertain and stressful. It was a period when, either through blind optimism or self-delusion, many people refused to believe that Britain could be going to war again, less than twenty-one years after the conclusion of the First World War. And most galling of all, the next war was going to be fought against the same enemy.

COUNTDOWN TO WAR

As early as 1932, the Deputy Prime Minister, Stanley Baldwin, pessimistically pronounced, 'I think it is well for the man in the street to realise that there is no power on earth that can protect him from being bombed, whatever people may tell him. The bomber will always get through.' Baldwin, by this time, knew that the so-called German Air Sports Association (*Deutscher Luftsportverband*) had morphed into the Luftwaffe (literally 'air weapon') and was training pilots in Russia of all places.

Eleanor Frost kept a diary for most of the war. Research shows that she was a very wealthy widow living with her daughter and elderly mother in Leigh Woods, a leafy suburb of Bristol. Eleanor Frost's wealth came from the family business, Frost & Reed: 'Art dealers since 1808 with offices and galleries in London's Mayfair and New York'. To confirm the source of her considerable wealth, **Eleanor** wrote in her diary on 8 September 1939, 'The Annual General Meeting of Frost & Reed today – a dividend of 5% on ordinary shares. Not bad considering the alarms and excursions of the last year.'

Bridge House in Leigh Woods, Bristol, where **Eleanor Frost**, her mother and daughter and many servants, lived for most of the war.

On 17 January 1938, **Eleanor** wrote:

Today I went to the first class of the Anti-Air Raid Course given for Clifton women. Miss Hall-Houghton is the moving spirit. She painted a grim picture of the possible suddenness and awfulness of war from the air. Well, if we all know all we can, it will make us an instructed public, less liable to panic and possibly useful.

Significantly, this was written more than a year and a half before the declaration of war.

On 10 February, she wrote, 'Saw *A Star is Born*. Went as a relief from these Gas Air Raid Precaution lectures and gas mask drill which seem a bit of a strain whilst I am also having my teeth out – two together.'

On 28 March she was much more optimistic about the political developments that day: 'The international situation seems immensely improved. In Mr Chamberlain's speech he shows great statesmanship, courage with caution, tenacity of purpose with a sense of appropriate firmness.'

Chamberlain, at this time, dominated the political stage in Britain. With his grizzled moustache, prominent teeth and quaintly reassuring starched wing collar, he was determined to pursue a policy of appeasement with Germany. But he was probably not just an out-of-touch old gentleman with a furled umbrella who, in Harold Nicolson's words, 'flew off to see Hitler with the bright faithfulness of a curate entering a pub for the first time'. He made the judgement that Britain had to buy time, however humiliating this policy might be.

From here on, preparations for war gathered pace. The people of Bristol, the author's home city, were advised to identify cellars, basements, church crypts, tunnels and caves suitable for use as air-raid shelters. In addition, public shelters were also built in many cities. Many people, however, distrusted these and chose to use them as rubbish dumps or public toilets. They very soon smelt strongly of urine.

★ ★ ★

Of all the women I interviewed who were old enough to remember this period, most spoke of dreading another war and their desperation to keep the peace. **Hazel Bray**, from Ashburton in south Devon, who was born in 1920, was warned by her father about the threat of war very early on:

He'd been a sailor in the Royal Navy in the First World War. But he died young, in 1932, when I was only 12. But I'll always remember what he said to me just before he died, 'I'm afraid you're going to have to live through another war. I won't, but you will'. And that was nearly nine years before war was declared!

Hazel Bray.

The pseudonymous diaries of another Bristol woman, who I will call '**HJF**' to preserve her anonymity, give telling insights into what women were thinking, doing and feeling at this time. She wrote in the introduction to her diary, 'To the generation of women yet to come, I offer this my diary, which gives some slight insight of how a very ordinary Bristol housewife lived in the years 1938 to 1945.'

On 26 August 1938, she wrote, 'The news this evening seems brighter. I think we shall all be so thankful to get something definite. The uncertainty is killing.'

Then on 14 September:

War seems inevitable. Prime Minister Neville Chamberlain is flying to see Hitler. Has the great British nation to wait upon an upstart like him? Where are our great men of the Victorian era? Made some more jelly. In case of war I must stock my larder with all the preserves I can make.

Almost two weeks later, on 27 September:

N. came. He was in very low spirits as he fears war is coming. He certainly knows its horrors as he was gassed in the last one. We listened to Mr Chamberlain on the wireless making every effort for peace.

This was the so-called Munich Agreement, when Chamberlain flew to Germany three times in two weeks for talks with Adolf Hitler. Hitler, in contrast, never once visited Britain. Chamberlain finally returned from Munich with a piece of white paper, which he waved theatrically, and pronounced that it meant 'Peace for our time'. He was then driven straight from Heston Airport to Buckingham Palace and five minutes later, he and his wife were standing on the balcony, waving, with the king and queen by their side – an unprecedented honour for two 'commoners'.

But Chamberlain's return wasn't universally well received. Some 15,000 people protested against the agreement in Trafalgar Square on 1 October, and one Labour politician, Hugh Dalton, suggested that the piece of paper that Chamberlain was waving was 'torn from the pages of *Mein Kampf*'.

While this was happening in London, **Hazel Bray** was at a teacher-training college in Salisbury:

> I remember the principal of the college interrupted Vespers to announce to all of us that, as a result of Chamberlain's agreement with Hitler, there wasn't going to be a war after all. But I didn't believe her. I knew we were just buying time, a year perhaps, before war was declared. It was inevitable.

Several other women referred to the Munich Agreement. **Diana England**, for example, said:

> My mother was so delighted when Chamberlain came back from Munich and proclaimed 'Peace in our time!' that she gave each of her three children a book – the *Oxford Book of English Poetry*. But she also said that, as much as she disliked Hitler, she detested 'those frightful Bolsheviks even more'.

Diana's mother had good reason to be worried about the possibility of a second war against Germany. Her husband had been wounded twice in the First World War, had a disfiguring facial wound and a piece of shrapnel buried in his stomach.

Joan Poole had this to say:

> I didn't really believe that it would come to war. We believed that Chamberlain would find a way of averting it. And we were right, for a time at least. And anyway, I don't think I worried too much about things like war. Like most girls of my age, I was far more interested in make-up and having a good time.

Dr Mary Jones was a medical student at the time:

During the 1930s I was fully aware that a war was probably imminent – that there was trouble ahead. But when Mr Chamberlain came home from Munich, I thought, like a lot of other foolish people, that that would be the end of it. But, of course, it wasn't.

On 30 September, **HJF** wrote:

Daddy arrived home at 4 a.m. from Fry's factory. He says he was on a machine that fixes bands on the gas masks … Is this war, and will our lives be constantly upset like this? ['Daddy' was the name **HJF** always used to refer to her husband.]

Another piece of forward planning was the possible evacuation of children. On 1 October **HJF** wrote:

Replied to Jean's [her daughter] Headmistress's leaflet re. sending children away from Bristol should war break out. We decided as Jean was nearly 14 years of age and she does not want to leave, to let this question rest for the time being.

As it turned out, Jean never was evacuated and, as a much-loved only child, she is often referred to in **HJF**'s diaries.

Diana England was sent away to boarding school at a young age and there, she admitted:

I was very cocooned, with very little contact with the outside world. We weren't even allowed to walk into the local village or listen to the wireless so I really knew very little about the impending war. But I do remember that my headmistress mentioned to us girls that she'd visited Germany during the school holidays and had been alarmed at the number of German military planes she saw.

Ruby Spragg was a working-class girl from central Bristol:

My father, Harry Davis, had been in the regular army for twenty-five years. He was always a military man who marched rather than walked. Anyway, after the First World War, he served in the British Army of Occupation and this convinced him that they would 'rise again'. And he was right, of course. But he also used to say to me, 'No one will ever beat us at war and they'll pay for it if they try.' In fact, he used to regularly go on and on about it to my mother in the kitchen. I don't think she listened half the time. She just used to get on with her cooking or the washing up.

Another thing I remember – when Hitler came to power, my father always referred to him as 'that bloody little corporal'. He himself had been a regimental sergeant major so he knew all about ranks in the army.

As a young girl, I suppose I listened to my father and believed what he said, especially when he said, 'The Germans will never invade this country. And they'd never defeat us. Never!'

Joan Fell, from Exmouth in Devon, said:

In 1938 I was at school and I remember at the time there were quite a few German boys in Exmouth, supposedly on holiday. I met some of them and they were friendly and polite, but I wonder now whether they'd been sent to snoop around the place – there was, after all, an important Marines base just up the road at Lympstone.

This anxiety was echoed by **Hazel Bray**:

We had two Geography teachers, a husband and wife, Mr and Mrs Peddoe. They weren't English, they came from somewhere in Eastern Europe. Anyway, we didn't like them, and one day, in the middle of a Geography lesson, a Military Police officer came into our class and spoke to the Peddoes and then ordered two military policemen to put handcuffs on them and arrest them. It was the last we saw of them. We assumed they must have been spies and as a result they were probably shot. I can't say we were sorry.

Like **Joan Fell**, **Diana England** also came into contact with young Germans of her own age:

We had some German girls at our school for a term. They spoke extremely good English I remember, and one of them, her name was Griselda, said to me when we were talking about the possibility of war, 'I don't want to fight you, Diana.' She then offered to shake my hand and I let her.

Rose Jennings was born in 1920 and had this to say:

> Towards the end of the 1930s, the talk was almost always of the imminent war, of how it was bound to come in the end. My father was a Rotarian and some German Rotarians came to stay with us and they told us about what it was like living under Hitler. When Chamberlain came back from Munich, I was convinced that it hadn't settled matters, that Hitler wasn't likely to abide by the terms of their agreement. I think, though, that other members of my family tried to push it to the back of their minds. But I couldn't and I was the one who measured up our windows for blackout curtains. The rest of my family used to laugh at me, I remember.

Iris Gillard had her own thoughts about the political situation at that time:

> I didn't think war was inevitable. I thought George VI was a wise and interesting man and he might somehow help to prevent it. But then Chamberlain came back from Munich and said, 'Peace in our time!' I just thought he was a gullible fool … By that time, I was certain war was coming. As for Hitler, I thought he was a dreadful little man, and in some ways I couldn't wait for the war to start. The sooner we got rid of him the better!

During this period, **HJF** wrote frequently in her diary about the imminent war:

> 3 February 1939: An Air Raid Warden called at 9.30 tonight to try the size of the gas masks we shall require. All of us take a medium size. Please God we shall never use them.

> 19 March: There was a meeting of the English cabinet last night to consider Romania's SOS to us. Picked primroses and violets in 'our lane' in Banwell.

A week later she first mentioned her interest in getting some sort of job in preparation for the war that now seemed almost inevitable:

> 27 March: ARP [Air Raid Precautions] asks all women drivers to send in their names for ambulance-driving, if necessary, so sent in mine.

In April, war preparations were becoming more pressing:

14 April: Went to the Whiteladies Picture House to see the ARP film 'The Warning', showing what things would be like in the event of war and air raids. Makes me very sad and depressed.

20 April: To an ARP lecture for ambulance drivers. I was given a First Aid Handbook. I do hope they will not expect me to bandage the injured as well as drive the ambulance.

27 April: The ARP lecture on the Circulation of the Blood, First Aid Treatment and wounds by pressure and tourniquet (the latter not to be applied round the neck!) and also on the treatment of fractures. I am getting bewildered!

4 May: Attended a third ARP lecture. Feel that the lifting of the stretcher with another member of the class on it is too heavy for me.

2 July: Had a picnic tea of raspberries and cream at Charterhouse. Listened to Mr Chamberlain on Air Raid Precautions.

A month later, **HJF** and her family had their last holiday together, on the Scilly Isles:

7 August: We went together to a lecture on Birds and Flower Life in the Islands. Talking to a woman inhabitant there she seemed to dislike England and the English for when the question came up as to whether there was going to be another war she said to me, 'England makes the war and expects us to send our men to fight for her.' I was shocked at her attitude.

25 August: I have been notified that I have been listed to serve as an Ambulance Driver at the Bedminster Division depot and that I am to report for duty when a message arrives, should war break out. These are anxious days.

But back to the war preparations of **Eleanor Frost**:

5 July: We are busy completing our preparations for the 'civil defence'. The dugout is finished and now it only has to be fitted with the necessary

stores and equipment. I am doing this and supervising the month's supply of food in the house which we are all asked to have. Mother is supervising the effective dark screening of all windows.

On 4 August she wrote succinctly, 'A quarter of a century since the start of the Great War.' Later that week, **Eleanor** went on holiday to Cornwall with her daughter Edith and her elderly mother, staying in a smart hotel overlooking the sea in Polzeath. There was only one problem with the hotel: 'They are feeding us too much meat and far too little fruit. My inside is barely functioning even with air evacuant.'

She was now closely monitoring the worsening international situation and so, apparently, were some of her fellow guests:

7 August: The crisis has become more and more acute and today about half a dozen people left on that account. I still do not believe it will develop into war.

On 26 August, **HJF** wrote, 'The war news is very grave. Hitler's letter to us is not yet published. Out in car and saw sandbags and sentries outside the Filton aeroplane works.'

It was on this day that many kerbs in central London were being painted white, the twelfth-century stained glass was being removed from Canterbury Cathedral and the National Gallery was closed while its pictures were being taken down, for 'safe-keeping' in a quarry in Wales.

27 August: Received another letter saying that I must be prepared for duty, day or night. I bought several tins for storing in the event of war. The news this evening seems brighter. I think we shall all be so thankful to get something definite; the uncertainty is killing.

At the end of August, things were going from bad to worse. On 31 August, **Eleanor Frost** wrote:

Things look black internationally. Walked to Port Quin and while there the wireless was switched on in a cafe and Edith heard, 'Consider that the war is inevitable.' She came back and told me – we both felt firm and calm but awful inside. Determined not to tell Mother until after lunch.

Later, **Eleanor** added, 'To our unbounded relief the whole sentence had been "We do *not* consider" etc.'

On 1 September, she wrote, 'A gorgeous hot day. But at 1 p.m. came the news that Germany has invaded Poland. People began to leave our hotel in the afternoon and several very late and again early on Saturday morning.'

In fact, German tanks and motorised troops numbering 1.5 million men crashed through the frontier between Germany and Poland at 4.58 that morning.

Eleanor's diary entry for 2 September reads, 'It is very empty and quiet in the hotel and on the beach.' And on 3 September:

> We planned to leave at 10.30 but discovered we had a puncture at the last moment. We left ultimately at 11 and reached home at about 6. We arrived to an empty house and had to get food and extemporise 'dark' lights, make beds and so on. At 10 p.m. we were all completely tired out.

It's perhaps curious that this was the day war was finally declared and yet **Eleanor** makes no mention of the fact.

Meanwhile, **HJF** was at home in Bristol:

> 2 September: Ambulance duty. Dreadfully bad weather and came home in complete blackout. Spent some time while on duty making black paper masks with cut slits for head and side lights of cars, according to the new regulation.

She then added ominously, 'We are still awaiting Hitler's reply.' She didn't have to wait for long.

THE DAY WAR WAS DECLARED

The historical background to the final declaration of war is as follows. On Friday, 1 September, the day Germany invaded Poland, Adolf Hitler broadcast his declaration of war with these words:

> The Polish state has refused the peaceful settlement of relations which I desired ... In order to put an end to this lunacy I have no other choice than to meet force with force ... The German Army will fight the

battle for the honour and the vital rights of a newborn Germany with hard determination.

To all intents and purposes, the Second World War had begun.

At 9 a.m. on Sunday, 3 September, the British ambassador to Germany, Sir Nevile Meyrick Henderson, went to the German Foreign Ministry. Henderson was a friend and admirer of Hitler's second in command, Hermann Goering. They shared a love of shooting. Henderson handed in an ultimatum which stated that unless the British Government received 'satisfactory assurances that Germany was prepared to withdraw from Polish territory, His Majesty's Government will without hesitation fulfil their obligation to Poland'. And this is what finally triggered Chamberlain's declaration of war at 11.15 a.m.

★ ★ ★

What did the women I interviewed remember of this historic announcement?
Ivy Rogers was 13 at the time:

Some of my family were at church but I was at home with my father. When I heard the news, I felt sick! I didn't want a war. Nobody wanted another war. It was terrible news. Of course, some people said it would be over by Christmas. How wrong they were.

Iris Gillard said, 'I think we felt a kind of relief when war was finally declared. Now we really knew what was happening. But I certainly didn't expect it to last for so long!'

Betty Gough was only 9. Her parents owned a sweet shop in Coventry. 'I remember a lady came into our shop looking very disturbed. She announced that war had been declared between Britain and Germany. I could tell by my mother's solemn expression that this was serious.'

Audrey Swindells was 11. She wrote in her memoirs:

Sunday the 3rd of September was a gloriously warm day and while my mother was making dinner I was in the garden when my father called out, 'Come in at once! The Prime Minister is to speak on the radio.'

My parents and my auntie looked very serious as we sat down. As Mr Chamberlain announced that we were at war, I couldn't really comprehend what being at war meant. But when the Prime Minister finished speaking I looked at my father. All the colour had drained from his face. 'It's only 21 years,' he said solemnly, 'and they told us that the last one was the war to end all wars.'

In contrast, **Enid King** said:

Audrey Swindells with her parents.

I was 15 and I was playing with some friends in the local park when my mother came out to tell us the news. It didn't mean much to me at the time. I was only a child really, despite the fact that I'd left school and started work.

Doris Marriot was also unfazed, 'I just thought it was all rather exciting.' **Hazel Bray**, who was 19 and a trainee teacher, was far more concerned:

When Chamberlain made his announcement, we all knew that this war wasn't going to be like the First World War because the civilian population was going to be involved, not just men in the services. And for this reason, we knew it was going to be a long and terrible war. I felt awful.

Dorothy Sanders was also a teacher:

We could all see it coming – or perhaps it's easy to say that with hindsight. Anyway, listening to Chamberlain and his speeches, he had really put us in a position where we didn't have any choice. We had to keep our promises to Poland, in particular. That's what treaties are all about.

Lorna Green was living in the small village of Carhampton, near Minehead in Somerset. She had just started work as a nurse. She wrote in her memoirs:

I was told that when war was declared – it was no longer 'if' – I should report to Minehead Hospital. So on September 3rd I was ready. I dug up potatoes to relieve the tension of waiting for Chamberlain on the wireless.

The announcement was made. I changed into my uniform and felt quite important cycling through the village to Minehead. Not all the villagers had heard Chamberlain but they knew war had been declared as they saw me cycle past.

Eleanor Frost didn't write anything on the day itself, but curiously waited until two days later:

5 September: Time at last to write in my diary. Our holiday in Polzeath actually ended only 3 days ago. It seems like a hundred years! We saw on a placard between Polzeath and Launceston 'War declared' and everywhere as we passed through the little towns we saw Territorials and Militia, some of them looking so young, far too young for war.

Many women associated the declaration of war with going to church. **Pam Allcock** remembered:

Halfway through the service, the vicar announced that war had been declared. He paraphrased Chamberlain's speech and the whole congregation was stunned for a few minutes but then the service continued. I walked home with my mother and she had a very long face, and afterwards, at home, my friends came round to play, but because we understood from our parents that something terrible had happened, we decided not to play after all. In fact, we sat in our dining room and solemnly declared that we wouldn't play again until after the war was over!

Enid Beebee, living in Redruth, Cornwall, also went to church that morning:

On the day war was declared, I was in the Wesleyan Chapel – I went mainly for the social life! Some boys came in late to the service and made signs to us to tell us the news – that war had been declared. I remember feeling very afraid, very apprehensive at the time. We all thought the bombs would start falling on us immediately, although of course they didn't.

Joan Watkins was also a churchgoer:

I was wearing a hat, a coat and gloves – we all did in those days, although it was very warm. The announcement was obviously very important to my parents but it was all very remote to a 13-year-old girl and it didn't really mean much to me. I suppose, if anything, I was all for it because I just thought my life was pretty dull at the time – anything for a bit of excitement.

I really didn't have any common sense. I only thought about myself and how things like a war would affect ME. Although, come to think of it, I didn't think about the possibility of people being killed by the war. My mother, by contrast, was quite a timid person and she hated the idea of war and fighting. In particular, she hated the idea of her own children being in danger.

Ruby Spragg remembered:

My mother was terribly upset. She went into the kitchen and cried and kept repeating, 'God bless us, God bless us.' I suppose she was upset and fearful because she thought my only brother would be called up and have to go off and be killed. She was right, in a way. He was called up. But thankfully he wasn't killed.

Lorna McNab didn't go to church that morning:

I was sent to the pub round the corner, the Portcullis, to get some cider. It was a warm day and lots of houses had their windows open and cooking smells were wafting out. But the city was very quiet. I realise now that everyone was inside listening to the wireless and I could hear the same voice coming out of every open window – the sound of the Prime Minister, Mr Chamberlain, announcing the declaration of war. When I got home with the cider, my parents and grandparents looked very serious. However, they didn't

Lorna McNab.

want to worry me, so my mother said simply, 'God will provide. I've had words with him.' My mother was very religious and she prayed a lot. But I'm not sure that it really helped!

Sheila Kellard wasn't in church either:

We'd gone for a week's holiday in Weston-super-Mare with my parents [a seaside resort approximately 20 miles from Bristol]. I remember the three of us were walking on the Promenade but we could clearly hear Mr Chamberlain's voice on the radio. My parents and everyone else around us just stood there, rooted to the spot. Nobody spoke, nobody moved. There was complete silence apart from Chamberlain's voice. I didn't really understand what it was all about, but I knew intuitively that it was terrible news. Our holiday was cut short and we went back to Bristol immediately.

Joan Poole had a similar experience:

It was my mother's birthday and the whole family was in Weston-super-Mare when we heard the announcement on some loudspeakers. I had a very funny feeling in my tummy and my parents stopped walking for a few moments, trying to take it all in. Then I remember I thought that it just wasn't right to hear such terrible news on my mother's birthday.

Describing the immediate aftermath of the declaration of war, **Jean Moore**, who was living in London at the time, said:

I had to go into work that day, even though it was a Sunday. So I got on my usual bus but it hadn't gone more than half a mile when we heard the air-raid sirens going. It was a terrible shock. We couldn't believe it, so soon after that radio broadcast. So we all got off the bus, all the passengers plus the driver and the conductor, and went down into the nearest shelter. By this time, we all had our masks on – we'd been told over and over again how important our gas masks were.

Vera Bartlett said that just after Chamberlain's radio broadcast, 'We heard an air-raid siren and I thought that bombs and poisonous gas were going to start dropping at any moment. I remember we all panicked as we tried to put our gas masks on.'

Clara Edwards was living in London:

The scene was so peaceful, the gardens in the park so lovely and the people walking by the river so unperturbed and ordinary with their perambulators and dogs ... War seemed too archaic and remote a word to contemplate.

Joyce Turner summed up the general feeling of the women I spoke to. 'I was in our back garden listening to the birds singing when Chamberlain came on the wireless. The whole bottom fell out of our lives. Everything that we'd been planning for our future was out of the window.'

The 'Bore War' and then the Real War

On the day after war was declared, Britain was emphatically not overwhelmed by the sort of patriotic fervour that gripped the country at the beginning of the First World War. The mood in September 1939 was a feeling of resignation, foreboding and real fear.

The country didn't have to wait long before its first official war casualty was announced. On his normal beat in central London, Police Constable George Southworth noticed a light on in a third-floor window of a house in Harley Street. After knocking on the front door and failing to get a reply, he decided to climb up a drainpipe. Unfortunately, he fell, breaking his neck.

The so-called 'Phoney War', or 'Bore War' as some people called it, really started the day war was declared and then continued until May 1940. The French called it '*le drole de guerre*' (funny war) and the Germans the '*Sitzkrieg*' (armchair war).

To begin with, the population of Britain fully expected thousands of bombs to come falling down on them at any moment but, eventually, many people, accidentally on purpose, forgot to carry their gas masks and became relatively lax about the blackout in the absence of any bombers overhead. In addition, of the thousands of children who had been evacuated to the countryside from the big cities, over half of them returned home to their families since there didn't seem to be much point in staying away.

Eleanor Frost wrote in her diary on Monday, 4 September 1939:

It was a beautiful night outside with a brilliant moon and star shine. Leaning out I thought I heard the constant sound of guns and deduced an air raid. It was a dreadful feeling. To my dismay I found myself shivering and could not stop.

In fact, there were no air raids on Bristol until nine months later.

The rapid mobilisation of thousands of men affected even the quiet suburb of Leigh Woods, where **Eleanor Frost** lived:

6 September: Burwalls has been taken over by the Tank Corps and there are over 500 men in there. [Burwalls is a very large house in Leigh Woods, barely 50m from Bridge House, where Eleanor lived.]

8 September: Since the Tanks Corps moved in we get up to Reveille and go to bed to the Last Post! Companies of men march by in steel helmets. They whistle as they march and swing along in great spirits.

Other small changes began to intrude on **Eleanor's** life:

11 September: The electricity light bulbs changed from 100 to 25 watt to try and cut down our usage, as requested. It means I can't see to write this diary. We have decided to try and keep our car going until Christmas.

Eleanor had this to say about the political situation: 'We hear that the Russians have invaded east Poland while preserving their own neutrality. What bunkum! Russia and Germany are again at their historic meal of eating up Poland between them.'

In fact, post-war historians discovered that Poland was to be partitioned as part of the Molotov–Ribbentrop Pact, signed on 23 August 1939.

Also on 11 September, **HJF** wrote, 'Today a barrage balloon has been flying nearly over our house. It looks like a huge white elephant without any legs.' A week later, she reported, 'We counted 23 barrage balloons within sight of our kitchen door.'

★ ★ ★

As far as the politics of this period are concerned, Britain didn't exactly cover itself with glory. For all the fine words of solidarity from the British Government, absolutely no military assistance was given to their Polish allies. The German *blitzkrieg* continued relentlessly until, on 20 September, the British Government thought it best to send this message to the Polish Government, 'All the world is admiring your courage ... We, your allies, intend to continue the struggle for the restoration of your liberty.'

The mayor of Warsaw sent this message back to London, 'I feel entitled to make a new appeal to you. When will the effective help of Great Britain and France come to relieve us from this terrible situation? We are waiting for it.' The answer was, in effect, never realpolitik.

But within a week of the declaration of war, the first units of the British Expeditionary Force (BEF) had disembarked in France and were preparing to fight the German Army, which was at that time poised on the French and Belgian borders. **Eleanor Frost** witnessed at first hand the departure of the BEF to France. On 20 September, she wrote:

> Derrick [presumably a relative] has just rung up to ask if he and three other officers can come and have a bath before entraining tonight. They arrived at 8.40 twilight in an army car so well camouflaged it was difficult to see. They all had baths and then a big dinner, the best that cook could provide at such short notice. But one should give them all the best one has. They went off at about 10.30. They were going to Avonmouth to embark for France. God bless them.

As a postscript to this act of generosity, she later wrote:

> I have received a letter from Derrick in France. In it he writes that 'we all very much enjoyed our evening with you and wished it could have lasted longer as it was the last time we experienced any home comforts the memory of which will last with us for a very long time!'

On 27 September, **Eleanor** wrote:

> This once peaceful and quiet spot is very much changed. Every house is now full either of refugees or evacuees from London or billeted people. Khaki-painted lorries roar past, evacuee children scream to one another, foreign refugees pass in noisy groups speaking God knows what language.

But **Eleanor** was by no means negative about the big changes to her life:

> 30 September: It ought not to take a war to give all its slum children a holiday in the country and it ought not to need a war to make us talk to

each other on buses and invent our own amusements in the evening and live simply and eat sparingly and recover the use of our legs and get up early enough to see the sun rise. However, it *has* needed a war which is about the severest criticism our civilisation could face!

Meanwhile, **HJF** was still driving an ambulance. 'I found driving in the gas mask and wearing a tin hat with leather gloves and oilskin coat very warm work and was relieved to breathe freely at the end of the trial.'
On 17 September, she wrote:

We hear that they have sunk our aircraft carrier *Courageous*. We are told that our RAF is sinking enemy submarines. Civilization! But no people anywhere want this war. Hitler's insane ambition. The German people are in some cases to blame for being passive to his government of cruelty and hate.

And three days later:

Out in car and saw convoys of army transport all covered with nets, with pieces of green and yellow rags attached for camouflage. They were lined up awaiting, no doubt, shipment to France. May God bring the men who drive the vehicles back safely to England.

In fact, by 27 September 1939, the BEF had already shipped 21,424 vehicles to France and 36,000 tons of ammunition. By the end of June 1940, after the evacuation of Dunkirk, these vehicles were effectively all lost and the British Army had to re-arm itself all over again.
On 23 September **HJF** noted, 'Petrol rationing commences.' But then immediately she added, 'Out in car to Redhill to collect my eggs and a goose for Michaelmas.' (Redhill is a village 10 miles south of Bristol.)
By the end of the month, the bureaucratic realities of an all-out war were beginning to be felt:

29 September: We filled in our National Registration Form and Daddy as head of the household signed it.

1 October: Daddy is out all day today issuing the cards and collecting National Registration Papers. He has made a very special effort to see the old man who would not take in his Paper, and has convinced him that it

is no trick of the Government to get him moved or to pry into his private affairs.

As autumn turned to winter, the *Sunday Pictorial* (now the *Sunday Mirror*) had this to say:

> The war remains in a state of suspended animation in which there is not much animation and a declining quantity of suspense. Our cities have not been bombed to destruction. Our proud race has not been defeated by death from the skies, by plague, starvation or by mustard gas. There has been no tremendous list of casualties as we may have expected. The war indeed has turned out to be a 'very queer business altogether'.

★ ★ ★

The year 1940 started cold and got colder. With heavy snow and thick ice across the country, it was one of the harshest winters anyone could remember. **HJF** wrote on 1 January, 'The first day of the New Year! May God bless us all and bring Peace soon!'

The rather dreary Phoney War continued. Life was cold and comfortless, drab and dull. Rationing was starting to bite, although its rules and regulations were patchy. Clothes were still freely available – if you could afford them. In fact, austerity hadn't really affected people's lives yet.

The blackout was causing problems, though. Pedestrians were being regularly knocked down by cars, although bus passengers had things made slightly easier when new dim lights on buses made it possible for them to at least read newspaper headlines and count out their change to offer to the conductor. All in all, the blackout regulations caused much resentment because of their perceived lack of point. Why prepare for bombing raids when the Germans had yet to develop a bomber that could fly as far as Bristol and back to Germany?

But this 'bore war', the lull before the storm, would soon be looked back on with nostalgia. By Easter, the military situation was becoming more and more ominous.

On 10 May 1940, the real war just the other side of the Channel began and **HJF** commented very succinctly, 'Germany invades Holland and Belgium. Mr Chamberlain resigns his Premiership. The King has cancelled the Whitsuntide holiday.' The next day, the maverick politician Churchill seized the opportunity to replace Chamberlain.

HJF recorded on 13 May, 'It is reported that the Germans are dropping troops by parachute in Holland and Belgium.' In fact, it was on this day that Churchill addressed the House for the first time, with these memorable words, 'I have nothing to offer but blood, toil, tears and sweat.' He then spelt out his extremely ambitious war aims:

Victory – Victory at all costs, victory in spite of all terror, victory however long and hard the road may be ... Come, then, let us go forward with our united strength.

HJF's only diary entry for that day was:

13 May: Joyce has the first of her extra French lessons arranged with Madame F.

On subsequent days in May she wrote:

14 May: We are stated to be on the eve of a great battle. The Queen and Princess of Holland have arrived in London. The news from Holland is very grave.

16 May: An appeal has been made on the wireless for stretcher-bearers.

31 May: Our army is withdrawing from Dunkirk. The Navy is helping.

On the same day, **Eleanor Frost** wrote, 'The BEF has left France. All three services have shown matchless courage and endurance.'

The evacuation of the BEF began on 27 May. It was expected that only about 10,000 men would be saved. In fact, the evacuation succeeded beyond all expectations. Destroyers, which brought off most of the men, were aided by 860 smaller vessels of one sort or another – pleasure steamers, fishing boats, barges, tugs, lifeboats, river ferries and even one or two rowing boats.

When the evacuation ended, 200,000 British and 140,000 French troops had been brought back to England. Nevertheless, Dunkirk was undeniably a humiliating and very costly defeat.

Hazel Bray had vivid memories of the aftermath of Dunkirk. She was a student at college in Salisbury at the time:

In June 1940, some senior girls, myself included, were asked to go to the railway station in Salisbury as soon as possible. We were there to help the WVS [Women's Voluntary Service] who were meeting trains that were just arriving from the south coast ports and on those trains were troops who'd just been evacuated from Dunkirk. They were in a shocking state. They were the walking wounded and none of them were wearing proper uniforms, just a few rags. Some were still wet through and horribly dirty, many with filthy bandages soaked with blood. Some were shaking so much from the shock of what they'd been through they couldn't even hold a cup to their lips to drink. I did as much as I could to comfort them, saying things like, 'It's all right. You're home now.' But that's about all I could do really. I'll never forget that.

Meanwhile, in Kent, trains crowded with filthy and defeated soldiers just off the boats from Dunkirk had to stop frequently at signals and small country stations – every railway line going north from the coast was full to capacity with trainload after trainload of wounded and bedraggled troops. But when word got around, members of local voluntary groups hurried up to the waiting trains with cakes, biscuits, sandwiches, cups of tea and jugs of lemonade. Local pubs also supplied umpteen bottles of beer. It was a heroes' welcome, but these weary, filthy and dispirited troops were anything but victors.

Ruby Spragg had a similar experience to **Hazel Bray**:

I remember after Dunkirk that on my day off, I walked up to Eastville Park. And there I saw something that really shocked me – there were hundreds of tents all over the park and they were all shapes and sizes, not just army tents. I suppose that's all they could find for the thousands of troops that had come back from Dunkirk. And in and around those tents I saw the soldiers who'd managed to get back to England. They looked awful! Some of them were just in rags, very unkempt and filthy, many with bloody bandages round their heads. It was so very sad – they really looked like a defeated army. They didn't look like soldiers anymore, they had no weapons, just the filthy-dirty clothes they stood up in. And certainly, none of them were smiling or even attempting to look cheerful. They just looked defeated, there's no other word for it.

Of course, we were only told the official news and there were definitely no photographs in the papers of men like these. So seeing them like that was really shocking. But they weren't there long. They were all just sent back to their units, I suppose, to fight again.

It was at about this time that the Cabinet split over whether or not to sue for peace or keep fighting. Churchill managed to defeat the proposal, but only just.

Rose Jennings, originally from Belvedere in Kent, also remembered the dark, depressing days of the summer of 1940:

After Dunkirk, I was convinced that the invasion was coming and that Kent would be rapidly overrun by the invading German Army on its way to London. Then I imagined they would probably partition the country, east and west, a bit like they had in France, and living in Bristol, I would be cut off from my home and my mother. I was very close to my mother and when I left her after my first half-term holiday, I remember clearly watching her leaning over our front gate and waving as I walked away down the road to catch my train. And then I thought perhaps I would never see her again.

On 10 June, **HJF** wrote, 'Italy declares war on Britain and France.' And then on subsequent days:

13 June: The French have thrown the Germans back 5 miles but a large number of our troops are cut off from the main force in Normandy. It is said to be a smaller Dunkirk, and large numbers of our men have been taken prisoner. Large parties of London children left for the West today.

14 June: A very sad day, The Germans have entered Paris. M. Reynaud has appealed to Mr Roosevelt for aid, and asked him not to send same too late.

The occupation of Paris began at 5.30 a.m. on 14 June, when German tanks rumbled past the Arc de Triomphe, down the Champs-Élysées and on to the Place de la Concorde. Parisians watched in silence, their arms folded. In the Place de l'Opéra stood a solitary Citroen car with a big, symbolic '*À Vendre*' ('For Sale') sign on it. By the end of the afternoon, a swastika hung from the Arc de Triomphe. Meanwhile, back in Germany, Hitler gave the order that for the next three days the swastika flag was to be flown from all public buildings and church bells throughout Germany should be rung for a minimum of fifteen minutes.

In France, the government left Paris and took up residence in Vichy. In its place, Paris was governed by the German military and certain approved French officials.

On 18 June, **HJF** wrote, 'School concert cancelled owing to the bad war news. Mr Churchill broadcast at 9 p.m. "We fight on".' She omitted to mention another significant part of what he had said, 'The Battle of France is over. I expect that the Battle of Britain is about to begin.'

Eleanor Frost wrote on 23 June, 'This morning we heard that France has signed an armistice with Germany. Well, a Briton always fights best with his back to the wall.'

Hazel Bray remembered that summer:

At one time, a member of the Home Guard came knocking on our front door asking for my father, who wasn't yet home from work. 'Are you aware,' the Home Guard said to my mother, 'that the Germans have left Calais and are on their way across the Channel to invade us?' Of course, it was only a rumour but we really were that close to being invaded.

As proof of how jittery the whole country was at the time, a local resident reported that on one 8-mile journey to the south coast near Bognor Regis, he was stopped a total of twenty times at roadblocks manned by fellow members of the Home Guard.

Eleanor Frost wrote in her diary:

1 June: Today we went to Portishead [a seaside resort 8 miles from Bristol] and sat on rocks, having had tea first under the trees. But before that, we were stopped *twice* by soldiers with fixed bayonets asking to examine our registration cards. Added to which the names on all signposts have been obliterated and the Downs, just the other side of the Avon Gorge from where we live in Leigh Woods, are now covered with heaps of stones and rocks to prevent enemy aeroplanes landing there.

Sunday, 14 July: The Suspension Bridge is now being barricaded and a tank trap is being made. Several of the men working at these defences were not navvies at all but businessmen giving their Sunday up to it.

Lorna Green, who by this time was studying medicine at the University of Bristol, summed up this early stage of the war:

There was a lull after the start of the war – the so-called Phoney War – with a false optimism in Britain, exemplified by songs such as 'Run, Rabbit, Run' and 'We'll Hang up our Washing on the Siegfried Line'. But soon the German Army was sweeping through Europe and into France. I remember sitting on the front in Minehead, gazing at the sea, desolate at the thought of the fall of France.

The heroism at Dunkirk inspired us all but brought home the risk of invasion. Coastal defences were strengthened, prohibited areas such as the south coast announced and the Battle of Britain – the defence by our air force began and was ultimately successful, although at great cost.

So now the stage was finally set for the next, bloodier and more destructive phase of the war. What next for this country? Invasion? Gas warfare? Steady starvation by blockade? A massive bombing campaign? Or, possibly, defeat? There was one certainty, though. The war on the Home Front, in one way or another, was going to involve women just as much as men.

GAS ATTACK

HOW TO PUT ON YOUR GAS MASK

Always keep your
gas mask with you
—day and night.
Learn to put it on
quickly.
Practise wearing it.

1. Hold your breath. 2. Hold mask in front of face, with thumbs inside straps.
3. Thrust chin well forward into mask, pull straps over head as far as they will go.
4. Run finger round face-piece taking care head-straps are not twisted.

IF THE GAS RATTLES SOUND

1. Hold your breath. Put on mask wherever you are. Close window.

2. If out of doors, take off hat, put on your mask. Turn up collar.

3. Put on gloves or keep hands in pockets. Take cover in nearest building.

IF YOU GET GASSED

| BY VAPOUR GAS | Keep your gas mask on even if you feel discomfort. If discomfort continues go to First Aid Post |

BY LIQUID or BLISTER GAS			
1 Dab, but don't rub the splash with handkerchief. Then destroy handkerchief.	2 Rub No. 2 Ointment well into place. *(Buy a bit for your face now.) In emergency chemists supply Bleach Cream too.*	3 If you can't get Ointment or Cream within 5 minutes wash place with soap and warm water.	4 Take off at once any garment splashed with gas.

A warning of the dangers of a gas attack. (*Picture Post*)

2

Preparing for the Worst: Gas Masks, Shelters and the Blackout

GAS MASKS

By this stage of the war, the preparations that the government had been working on for a long time were now more or less in place. The manufacture and distribution of gas masks was an example of huge-scale forward planning. Working under immense pressure, a new factory in Blackburn, Lancashire, produced 'respirators', as they preferred to call them, on a very large scale. Just a month after the war had started, 38 million masks had been produced – enough for virtually every man, woman and child in the country. Ironically, we now know that wearing the masks was potentially dangerous because they contained a quantity of chrysolite in the filter, otherwise known as white asbestos, although at the time this wasn't known to be carcinogenic. This was only discovered years later, when workers in the factory started dying of cancer at an abnormally high rate.

As well as putting on a mask as soon as a gas attack was signalled, the following extra advice was given:

If you are out of doors you are advised to turn up your jacket collar to stop gas going down your neck.

Put on gloves or put your hands in your pockets to stop your skin being affected by gas.

The fear was that gas had proved such an effective weapon in the First World War, it would almost inevitably be used again in the Second World War. Gas canisters dropped from bombers were expected to have devastating consequences, particularly because the gas used would be far more potent and lethal. Accordingly, big posters on display everywhere carried the simple message, 'Hitler Will Send No Warning – so always carry your gas mask'.

Gas masks were made of rubber and wearing them was a hot and smelly experience. Air was sucked in, with some difficulty, through a filter and then breathed out under pressure round the sides of the mask. Children delighted in the farting noises they could make breathing out. They were fearsome to look at, too, transforming the wearer into some form of 'pig-snouted alien'.

Government-sponsored publicity for the new-fangled 'civilian respirators' was widespread. Cigarette cards, in particular, carried instructions on how to put them on: 'Remember, chin in – right in – first, before you start to pull the straps over your head.' And the basic government advice was repeated over and over again, 'Take care of your gas mask and your gas mask will take care of you.'

The signal to put on gas masks was a wooden rattle, often an old football rattle, sounded by air-raid wardens, while the signal for the 'All Clear' was a whistle. In the event of a gas attack, local swimming baths' changing rooms were designated for use as decontamination chambers.

In fact, people very rapidly became blasé about carrying gas masks, despite all the government propaganda. A survey in November 1939, only two months after the start of the war, revealed that on Westminster Bridge only 24 per cent of men were carrying their gas mask and 30 per cent of women, while in one town in Lancashire, the percentages were a paltry 6 per cent and 4 per cent respectively. All over the country, forgotten gas masks soon filled the shelves of railway lost property offices. And just to prove how everyone was becoming 'careless', in a 1942 film, *The Goose Steps Out*, a German spy is instructed on how to look as British as possible with the admonition, 'Whatever you do, don't ever be seen carrying a gas mask.'

★ ★ ★

Betty Jones collected her gas mask from a local village hall and after that:

We had to carry it hung over one shoulder, a bit like a handbag, every-where we went, to the shops, to work, at all times. I even had mine on a chair beside my bed when I went to sleep. And it became a sort of ritual to say every time I went out: 'Don't forget gas mask, identity card, torch.'

Sheila Kellard remembered, 'If we forgot to take our gas mask to school with us, we were sent home immediately to fetch it. For practise purposes, we even had one lesson with our masks on the whole time.'

Greta Cockaday was living in London at the beginning of the war. 'I went to work on the Tube. I don't think I bothered to carry my gas mask with me. I was young and I never thought anything bad could happen to me.'

Betty Jones who, unlike many people, always carried her gas mask.

Doris Marriot was also living in London:

I hated those gas masks because the bottom of my mask used to fill up with saliva and sweat. And another thing, the straps used to catch in my hair. And I loathed the smell and the feel of rubber – I always have done. I don't like rubber bands even today!

AIR-RAID SHELTERS

In addition to having to think about gas masks, preparing for the worst also meant learning to live with air-raid shelters. In November 1938, the government decided to provide as many families as possible with a shelter. Home Secretary Sir John Anderson ordered prototypes of a cheap, easily erected shelter to be designed and constructed. Two weeks later, the first prototype was produced and Anderson, a man of considerable weight, jumped up and down on its roof just to prove that it really worked.

It consisted of six curved sheets of corrugated and galvanised iron, bolted together at the top and with steel plates at either end, one with an opening over which a piece of material, usually an old sack or piece of carpet was hung. It was just big enough to accommodate six people, albeit not comfortably. Those taking shelter sat facing each other, their knees usually touching.

Lighting the Anderson shelters was a problem. Most people resorted to candles. As for heating, the government suggested hot-water bottles or bricks heated in the kitchen oven or homemade sleeping bags made from old blankets and stuffed with newspapers.

One perennial problem was that the shelters frequently became very muddy underfoot or even waterlogged.

Dogs were not officially allowed in shelters in case they went barking mad with the banging and crashing outside and bit their owners. In fact, over 400,000 dogs were put down by the RSPCA in London alone in the first weeks of the war and a captive bolt pistol was advertised for sale for this purpose. A field in Essex was designated a mass grave and over half a million dogs were buried there. Cats, on the other hand, were deemed relatively shockproof and were allowed into shelters, canaries and budgerigars likewise. Poisonous snakes in London's zoos were euthanized, just in case they managed to escape during a bombing raid.

But even if you did have an Anderson shelter in your back garden, there was no guarantee you would use it. **Ivy Crier** remembered:

> Our neighbours were very nervous of the bombs and they slept in our Anderson shelter every night. But funnily enough, we never did. We slept in our own beds. I used to say: if we go, we all go together in our own home.

Margaret Bowring described the prevailing attitude in the Dings, a working-class area in central Bristol:

> Many of our neighbours just used to shrug their shoulders and say, 'Shelters? What, dig a hole in our backyard and hide in a tin box covered in a bit of earth? No, thank you! Worse still, replace the dining room table with a metal box with wire sides and crawl into that? What do they think we are, animals in a zoo?'

The metal box **Margaret** was referring to was the Morrison shelter. The fact was, only 25 per cent of the British population had a garden or backyard big enough to erect an Anderson shelter. The other 75 per cent relied initially on communal shelters and then, later on, Morrison shelters. They were

A Morrison shelter ready for use at bedtime. (piemags/Alamy Stock Photo)

essentially metal cages with a steel-plate top or roof, designed to withstand the weight of a collapsed ceiling. The sides were made of wire mesh.

Morrison shelters had the great advantage that they could also be used as a table, although there was nowhere to put your knees. They were provided free to families with an annual income of less than £350. By the end of 1941, when the worst of the bombing was over, more than half a million had been distributed. In a survey of forty-four severely bomb-damaged houses, it was discovered that only three people had actually been killed and thirteen seriously injured out of a total of 136 people who were sheltering in Morrison shelters.

Some people had enough space and money to build their own substantial shelters in their gardens. **Eleanor Frost** called it their 'dug-out':

> 23 June 1940: This week I have completed the dug-out and now we have chairs, a screen, food, cards, a medicine chest, a stove and kettle, tea apparatus, soap and towels and all sorts of things such as candles, matches, Malvern Water and so on.

Soon after that she wrote, 'Mother now has enough food in the house and in the dug-out to be self-supporting for a fortnight. One wonders so much what the next few weeks will bring forth. Better not to wonder perhaps.'

★ ★ ★

Communal shelters were made of brick walls 14in thick and with a 1ft-thick, reinforced concrete roof. Up to fifty people could take refuge in them but unfortunately the walls weren't strong enough to withstand a powerful bomb blast and the roofs had a habit of collapsing on the occupants below.

THE BLACKOUT

There was also the blackout. This was first enforced on the night of 1 September 1939, two days before the declaration of war. Street lights all over the country were turned off and cars had to drive at walking pace in the pitch darkness. The number of road accidents that September more than doubled.

Ivy Rogers, who was 13 at the time, helped to put up the blackout in her house in Bristol:

> It was made of heavy, black material. We pinned it up over the window and then pulled the curtains after that. Funnily enough, I've still got some of that material upstairs now. Don't suppose I'll ever need it again!

Betty Jones remembered:

> If you left even a tiny chink of light showing, the warden would shout, 'Put that light out!' Or worse still, you could have a knock at the door and the warden could give you a good telling off.

The air-raid wardens who were responsible for enforcing these regulations were easily recognised by their navy blue uniform topped off by a tin helmet with a white capital 'W' on the front. A lot of people regarded them as jumped-up, interfering busybodies – 'little 'itlers', as some called them – others saw them as selfless pillars of the local community. To begin with, there were only a few women wardens but as conscription for almost all men came in, this number increased rapidly.

Eleanor Frost wrote on Monday, 4 September 1939, 'Spent the afternoon painting glass panels with black paint and doing curtains, etc. That night Mother, Edith and Margaret had severe sickness and diarrhoea and were up and down a great part of the night.'

On Wednesday, **Eleanor** 'was still very busy lining curtains with thick black stuff'. By Friday, 'Everywhere as one passes houses there is the sound of tapping, people tacking up cloth etc to screen lights'. And on Saturday, 'I think I have made the last pair of black curtains. We thought the house was ready before we went away but for the skylights, ventilators and peep holes and cracks of light still seem legion.'

In addition to blackout curtains, homeowners were instructed to protect themselves against potentially lethal flying shards of glass from shattered windows by criss-crossing every window with sticky tape, leaving no more than 6in of glass clear.

Putting up the blackout every night had to be done forty-five minutes before sunset, whenever that was, and the time was publicised in every newspaper and on every radio news bulletin. This daily chore could take anything between ten and forty-five minutes, depending on the size of your house.

Some people at the beginning of the war only thought it necessary to put blackout curtains over windows at the front of their house. Air-raid wardens soon taught them otherwise. During the course of the war, 925,000 people were fined for showing lights – the equivalent to one in fifty people – and in general, blackout regulations were strictly enforced. In West Wickham, Kent, a cyclist was stopped and subsequently fined £1 for having a front light that was too bright, despite the fact that it had a sheet of tissue paper over it. Most extreme was the case of a man fined for lighting his cigarette in the street.

The blackout also included all forms of motor transport. On 16 September, **HJF** wrote:

I took the car down to Henley's Garage to have the wings painted white. This is the custom now, as it shows up better in the dim lights of other cars in the blackout. I found driving in the blackout very trying. Spent some time while on duty making black paper masks with cut slits for head and side lights.

Driving and keeping to the newly introduced 20mph speed limit was difficult because dashboards couldn't be illuminated. You just had to judge your speed by the sound of the engine.

Lorna Green described one incident in the blackout:

At night headlights had to be almost completely obscured so night driving for me meant keeping to the middle of the road. Except one evening, I remember driving onto the top of a small roundabout, neatly balanced with all four wheels in the air. Fortunately, some passers-by helped with rocking and pushing the car until once more it reached the road. Unfortunately, the exhaust was badly damaged and the car roared very noisily all the way home.

Dr Mary Jones remembered:

Batteries for torches were in very short supply so we had to be very careful how much we used them. The torch that I used also had to be small, shrouded in tissue paper and I could only point it at the ground immediately in front of my feet.

HJF wrote in her diary on 14 October, 'Whitened the edges of our front steps which are very difficult to see in the dark. We are having to count them as we ascend.'

Because the blackout was so effective, some pedestrians risked walking in the middle of the road, following the painted white lines. Men were also advised to let their white shirt tails hang out so they could be more easily seen by other pedestrians. Nevertheless, a poll in January 1940 revealed that practically one person in five had sustained an injury, such as a twisted ankle or sprained wrist.

Vera Bartlett, living on her own as a single mother with her husband Ted away fighting in France, remembered one incident in the blackout, 'I was running to get home when the sirens sounded and it was so dark I ran straight into a policeman and fell flat on my face. He was very kind – he saw me home after that.'

★ ★ ★

Still on the subject of preparing for the worst, the government had, by this stage, requisitioned swimming pools and warehouses all over the country for use as emergency morgues. They had also secretly ordered the manufacture of hundreds of thousands of makeshift cardboard coffins.

So Britain was now prepared. It remained to be seen whether those preparations were necessary and, if so, how effective they would be.

Ted and **Vera Bartlett** just before they married.

3

For Safety's Sake:
Evacuees' Stories

Gas masks, bomb shelters and the blackout weren't the only examples of huge-scale and far-reaching forward planning by the government. They also planned the evacuation of 3 million children and pregnant women from Britain's industrial cities to the relative safety of rural villages all over the country.

This was a massive undertaking. On the first day of the evacuation, 1 September 1939, crowded trains left the capital's main stations every nine minutes — for nine hours! Some London children were even evacuated by ship down the Thames. This huge operation affected the lives, one way or another, of nearly all the women interviewed for this book.

On 31 August, four days before the declaration of war, the government ordered 'the biggest exodus since Moses' to be put into effect. The planning even involved the recording of a special lullaby, to be broadcast by the BBC every night just before bedtime. The first two lines read, 'Sleepy little eyes in a sleepy little head. Sleepy time is drawing near.' Sentimental actions such as this stand in stark contrast to many of the stories I was told.

On the day of the big evacuation, over 17,000 WVS members organised almost everything at ground level. This involved, among many other things, putting brown luggage labels round the necks of all children on which were written the child's name and school. The WVS then shepherded them, including many waifs and strays, onto hundreds of waiting buses and trains. As a matter of historical record, not a single child was lost during those two days.

After it was all over, a journalist described London as a 'childless' city. In fact, in the space of just a month, the percentage of the population of the capital under 10 years old had plummeted from 14 per cent to only 2 per cent.

Many children went much further away than the rural villages of the Home Counties or the West Country. Hundreds of thousands left the country and went to Canada and the US. **Eleanor Frost** described this exodus:

> Margery, waiting at Euston Station for her train, said that she had just seen a train leave for Liverpool laden with children and young people. The hustle and bustle in the station had to be seen to be believed. She reported that she heard one dear child, a little boy of about 5 with his mother, shout, 'Goodbye Daddy. I'll take care of Mummy for you!' The sight and sound of it all made my heart turn over.

Two days later, **Eleanor** wrote:

> The Yates's grandchildren have gone to Canada, alone. They will be met there by people longing to have them for the war and for always should anything happen to their parents here. Patrick is only 9 and Colin only 5! What self-reliant young men they should develop into.

But back to children who were being evacuated to families in this country. **Rose Jennings** was, at this time, not old enough to be a member of the WVS – she was still at a girls' grammar school in Kent – but she nevertheless volunteered to help:

> I went to the local station and then helped to look after the children on the train journeys to their new 'homes'. Some of them wanted to know where they were going but I had no more idea than they did because all the station signs had been removed. All I knew was that we were going out into the country, deep into rural Kent, away from danger.
>
> Some of those children were quite cheerful and in high spirits, as though they were going away on holiday. Others were terribly upset and in floods of tears. I just had to do my best to comfort them. I told them stories and played games with them. Anything to keep their spirits up. But I was only a schoolgirl myself!

Audrey Swindells, who was 11 at the time described her experiences in her memoirs:

> We were living in Birmingham and I remember getting on a train and lots of parents looking very sad. Some were crying, including my mother. But for me it felt like an adventure. I think we took our own sandwiches but I had nothing to drink and nor did anyone in my carriage. The weather was still very warm and the journey was quite long because we were frequently taken into sidings and stopped to let troop trains pass. We arrived at last, desperately thirsty. Thankfully, some adults met us on the platform with water and cordial drinks. From there we were taken to a church hall where people were going to choose us and I was chosen by a Mr and Mrs Buggins. Then me and another girl from my school called Cynthia Payne went in their car to their house where we met their daughter. She was also called Audrey!
>
> We five soon began to adjust to living together and we were made very welcome. We went to the local grammar school, but only half-time because Redditch Grammar School used their school in the mornings and we used it in the afternoons. The weather was still warm and I remember sitting in the garden writing home to my parents and because we were told at school to keep our letters home cheerful, I praised everything that was happening. Anyway, it must have been in December 1939 when one day the doorbell rang and Mrs Buggins, busy in the kitchen, asked me to answer it. To my astonishment it was my mother.
>
> 'I've come to take you away from here,' she said. And then suddenly there was Mrs Buggins with her arms on my shoulders saying, 'Who are you?'
>
> 'She's my mother,' I said.
>
> 'Well, you'd better come in. I wish you'd let me know you were coming,' said Mrs Buggins, with some justification.
>
> Turning to me as she walked in my mother said, 'Sorry I couldn't let you know dear, but will you go and get your things together because we have a bus to catch.'
>
> I was completely astounded as she added, 'Go along dear, please.' As I went up to the bedroom to get out my clothes, Mrs Buggins and my mother went to the sitting room. After a while I could hear shouting and Mrs Buggins crying out – which I'd never heard her do before – 'Birmingham! You can't take her to Birmingham – that's sure to be bombed. There are so many munitions factories there! Please leave Audrey here.'

'Certainly not. She must be back with her father and me – now.'

I was very distressed and couldn't understand my mother's behaviour. But in retrospect, the problem may have been my very positive descriptions of my new life with the Buggins and my mother seriously believing that I was growing away from her.

My final parting from the Buggins was chaotic. Cynthia and Audrey were both crying whilst my mother was in the bedroom putting my clothes in a case which she'd brought with her.

Then, as my mother took the case and my arm to leave the house, Mrs Buggins was saying, as she too was crying, 'This is outrageous!'

As I was pulled out of the garden gate I was looking back, horrified and embarrassed. I didn't even say goodbye properly to anyone or thank them for anything.

Patricia Roffe was also a child evacuee aged only 12:

I came from Rotherhithe, a dockland area in South East London. On the Friday, two days before war was declared, I was taken on a bus to the nearest station and then I went by train with my cousin Eileen, who was five years older than me, to Worthing on the south coast. When we got there, we were taken to a church hall where it was a bit like a cattle market.

We stood around in small groups with the children from our street or our school class and people called out, 'I want a girl' or 'I want two boys'. But I was determined to stay close to my cousin Eileen and luckily enough, a woman called Mrs Denyar agreed to have both of us. She then gave me a postcard to send home to my parents with her address on it.

Pat Roffe, who was evacuated from Rotherhithe in the East End of London when she was 12.

But unfortunately, the Denyars' house had only two bedrooms and they had a son of their own. This meant I had to share a small bedroom with Eileen and I had to climb over her to get to my bed, which was against the wall. I remember very clearly on the first night I was so nervous I was sick and the sick went all over my bed and Eileen and her bed. I was so embarrassed!

In fact, I didn't stay there very long at all. There was no bombing back home in London so after only about five weeks we both went home to Rotherhithe and stayed there for the rest of the war, all through the worst of the bombing!

Suzanne Best and all the pupils from her private girls' school in Portsmouth were also evacuated very early on in the war:

A few days after war was declared we were told that we were going to be moved to a big country house called Hinton Ampner in Hampshire. They told us it was owned by the 8th Baron Sherborne and he was going to live in one wing of the house while we girls, our teachers and classrooms occupied the rest of his house.

We were taken there by bus and I remember feeling very excited at the time as though I was going on a big adventure. I didn't take many clothes or possessions with me – everything I had was in one suitcase, just small enough for me to carry. Anyway, I'll always remember when we arrived, the butler, wearing a green, baize apron, was halfway up a stepladder still endeavouring to take down an enormous chandelier.

Suzanne probably had plenty of clothes to take with her but working-class children often didn't. Their parents were issued with a long list beforehand, which included a gas mask, of course, a change of underwear, pyjamas or nighties, plimsolls or slippers, toothbrush, comb, towel, soap, face flannel, six handkerchiefs and a warm coat. Some parents reportedly found it difficult to supply many of the things on the list. A coat? Pyjamas? Handkerchiefs? A nightie? A spare pair of shoes? And most onerous of all, a toothbrush?

Suzanne Best.

Many working-class children had never had such a thing, let alone used one. **Suzanne Best** continued:

I was only 9 but life at this girls' boarding school was fun in many ways. We girls became very close. I suppose we provided mutual support for each other. I don't think I missed my parents particularly and I don't remember feeling homesick.

Janet Allport was from a working-class family in Bristol:

We'd been bombed out of our home so we had nowhere to live. But soon after that, we were told that Mr Churchill had decided we needed a holiday in the country, away from all the bombing. It wouldn't be for long, we were told. So there we were, standing on the station platform, with me carrying a lime green suitcase with brown leather corners. In it were all my clothes, but no toys, not even a doll or a teddy bear.

Mum's last words to us were, 'Don't let them split you up. Stay with your two sisters whatever happens.' Then a bossy woman in a felt hat pushed us onto the train. We were scared and I think a lot of us were crying but then I fell asleep. When we got to Crediton station, we were shepherded into a big hall and told to take our clothes off, all except for our navy blue knickers. Then nurses in big, white hats came round with enamel bowls full of disinfectant and examined us. In particular, they checked our hair for head lice.

It was a sad fact that many of the evacuee children came from desperately poor, inner-city slums and it was soon discovered that many suffered from scabies and/or impetigo and head lice. Some had never worn underclothes, let alone underclothes that had been recently washed, and many had never sat down at a dining table to eat a proper meal.

One perhaps apocryphal story involved a young mother with her 6-year-old son arriving at the relatively grand home of a genteel lady. The son urinated on the carpet in the middle of the sitting room. 'You dirty thing, messing up the lady's carpet. Go and do it in the corner!' was reportedly the mother's response.

Janet continued her account of being evacuated from Bristol to Devon:

When we eventually got to the small village of Cheriton Fitzpaine, us three sisters were determined to stay together and we clung to each other. But a woman called Mrs Brewer said, 'Who would like to come with me?' and, silly me, I said, 'Me!' That was a terrible mistake, it turned out, because that's how we became separated. Muriel and Myrtle went to stay on a farm and I went to live in a cottage in the village on my own. I cried and cried, I remember, and night after night I sobbed myself to sleep.

The couple I lived with, Mr and Mrs Brewer, had no children and they had no interest in me as a child. They treated me as a thing and they cared much more for their dog than me. I remember I wanted to go and see my sisters Muriel and Myrtle and Mrs Brewer said to me, 'You're not going.' 'But I want to!' I screamed. And then she slapped me.

One of the worst things was how hungry I became. Myrtle and Muriel had as much jam and cream for tea as they liked but I only had burnt toast. I was so jealous of them! I even tried eating some soil, I was that hungry. Nothing made me smile while I was there. I was really, really unhappy.

Janet's younger sister **Myrtle** had this to say:

I was just 5 at the time and I remember there was a real hullabaloo in our house on the day we left. My mother was terribly upset. She came with us to the station but my father didn't – he was at work. He was a docker. Although she was a strong woman she was fighting back the tears, although we couldn't understand why. As we waved her goodbye, the last words she spoke were, 'Look after our Myrtle.'

But in the village of Cheriton Fitzpaine, we were separated because there were no families in the village who wanted three children. We were sent to live on a big farm, Barns Hill Farm, it was called, with Mr and Mrs Sparks. It was an enormous old house with two staircases and we used to run round and round, up one staircase and down the other.

While I was there I was even given a pet of my own. It was a yellow ferret but it had terribly sharp teeth and it was spiteful and it bit me. They used my ferret to catch rabbits, but luckily I didn't have to kill the rabbits myself.

While I was there I pretended to help on the farm. I remember I ran around with a pitchfork a lot – but I was probably more of a hindrance than a help. I was only 5, after all, and just attention seeking. I've always been a bit like that!

While I was there, we were very well fed. When you lived on a farm, like we did, you weren't really affected by food rationing. We had plenty of milk and eggs and bacon – and rabbit meat, of course.

We went to the village school, next to the church. It was a lovely school. I was in the 'little ones' class – there were only two classes in the school. Anyway, I remember thinking, 'Why do we need to go to school? We're only here for a short holiday.' Little did we know … Meanwhile, my sister Janet was having a miserable time. We used to meet her every day before school. She was so unhappy!

Another Bristol girl, **Aisla Marshall,** had a very different experience to poor **Janet**. According to **Myrtle**:

She was staying with a lovely family in the village who didn't have any children of their own and she was so happy there she didn't want to go home, and as far as I know she never did. I think the family in Cheriton Fitzpaine must have adopted her.

In fact, she was left the cottage she lived in and she later married the village postman, Arthur Blisset. **Aisla** was still living in that cottage when she died in 2020 and her son, Ian, still lives there now – an evacuee's story which had very long-term results.

Myrtle continued:

Our mother was only able to come and visit us twice the whole time we were there and she never wrote letters to us – she didn't have time. Anyway, we didn't know she was coming and she only stayed for half a day. We asked over and over again, 'When can we come home?' but she could never answer that question because I suppose she had no say in the matter. She just had to wait until the authorities decided what should happen to us. And in the end that took a whole eighteen months!

I missed my mother dreadfully and I remember I often used to cry myself to sleep at night. Eventually, my dad said he'd had enough, they're coming home. We were so happy! And when we got back, there were all our friends still alive so we needn't have gone away at all.

Joyce Biggs, who was also from Bristol, went even further west than **Janet** and **Myrtle** – to Cornwall. She also described what happened to her in great detail:

Me and my brother were taken to Temple Meads station and put on a train to 'somewhere in the West Country'. I was scared, of course I was, leaving home for the first time and not knowing when, or even if, I was going to see my parents again. But things got better after that because on the train I met my best friend from school, Evelyne Boyle, and we stuck together for the whole journey.

We eventually got off at Falmouth station and were then taken on a bus to a tiny Cornish village called Helford Passage. There I went to stay with a lovely couple called Mr and Mrs Williams. Their cottage was very small with only two bedrooms, so my brother had to stay in the cottage next door with another couple. Evelyne also stayed in Helford Passage.

I remember the Williams' cottage only had an outside toilet and no electricity, only candles. There was definitely no bath. But Mr and Mrs Williams were extremely kind to me. Mr Williams was a fisherman and his name was Bill, I remember. He had his own small fishing boat, a rowing boat, and he used to go fishing for mackerel and lobsters mainly. He took us out with him in his boat sometimes. He even let us borrow it, so me and my friend Evelyne tried to row it but we just went round in circles.

There was also a lovely beach across the road from us where we used to go swimming. It really felt like we were on holiday, although to get to that beach we had to crawl under some barbed wire – there was a lot of barbed wire all along the coast. I suppose they thought there might be an invasion even down in Cornwall.

There was one small problem though – Helford Passage didn't have a school so we had to walk 5 miles to a school called Mawnan Smith School in another village. [In fact, that school was only 1½ miles away.] But we didn't mind walking, not really.

And we got to know a lot of people in the area. Many of them lived on farms – they were very kind, friendly people down there and I got on well with the other local children at school and the bombing in Bristol seemed a long, long way away. In fact, while I was down there in Cornwall you wouldn't really have known there was a war on.

My parents came to see us twice while we were there. They came by train, there and back the same day because they definitely couldn't afford a hotel for the night. I think my mother stopped worrying about us when they saw how happy we were. In fact, I think I worried more about her back in Bristol than she did about me.

Looking back on it now, I was homesick of course and I missed my parents but not enough to make me unhappy. To be honest, I don't think I really wanted to go home.

Joyce Grant was also sent away from Bristol when the bombing got really bad, to stay with some relatives of her father who came from a Welsh mining family:

> Those mining towns and villages were never really bombed. The only problem was my aunt's house – it was only very small. That meant I had to share a bed with four other girls – my two sisters and two cousins. It was very, very crowded!
>
> While I was there I went to the local village school and I had to learn Welsh. Even the boys who'd been evacuated from London also had to learn Welsh. Funnily enough, I can still remember a few words even today.

Audrey Stacey was bombed out of her house in Bristol and was sent away to live in a small cottage in the village of Bitton about 5 miles away:

> It only had an outside toilet in a shed at the bottom of the garden. It was really only a wooden seat over a bucket! The flies and the smell were disgusting and we had to share it with the people living next door.
>
> While we were there, I went to the village school. It was very small – it only had two classes. The headmaster taught the top class, the one I was in, and his wife the other class.
>
> I'll always remember one thing that happened to me at that school. One day in class, the headmaster grabbed me by the collar and dragged me to the front of the class and shouted, 'How dare you bring this filthy trash into my school?' He then said he'd been told that I'd been seen reading a book by Ruby M. Ayres. I thought it was terribly unfair because I'd never even heard of Ruby M. Ayres. I much preferred a magazine for girls called *Girls' Crystal*! [Ruby M. Ayres wrote 135 novels which were comparable to books nowadays published by Mills & Boon. They were anything but salacious, but the headmaster presumably thought that this girl from the big city of Bristol was a threat to the innocence of the village children.]

Audrey Stacey.

Many other evacuee children described a contrast in living conditions. The daughter of a well-to-do Bristol vet, **Pam Allcock**, was living in a large house in Clifton before her family were bombed out. She and her brother were then sent to live with her Uncle Clem in Maidenhead:

> We lived there for about six months with my aunt and uncle. He was the headmaster of an elementary school but for some reason he didn't think his school was suitable for me and I spent the next six months on holiday from school. That was probably illegal but nobody had time to check on that sort of thing.
>
> It was far more crowded than at home in Bristol – as well as my brother Pat and I and their two sons, they had another evacuee, a boy called Len from London. Funnily enough, I still keep in touch with him more than seventy-five years later!
>
> There was no inside bathroom in that house and we had only one bath a week, in a zinc tub under the table. We didn't eat so well in Maidenhead either, but I do remember that my Uncle Clem, headmaster, lay reader and pillar of the community, once bought a black-market haunch of venison from a man in a pub. Presumably, it was part of a deer poached in Windsor Great Park, which was nearby. I worried that the king would hear about it and come to claim back his deer and punish us. I was still quite young at the time!

Barbara Steadman was also from Bristol:

> I was evacuated with my older sister Janet to the small village of Holsworthy in Devon. I'll never forget the time I spent there, although I suppose I was only 5 at the time.
>
> We lived in a very small cottage which had no electricity – we were dependent on paraffin lamps for lighting – and no running water. We had to walk 500 yards with a bucket to get water from a well! And that water was rationed because it took so much time and trouble to fetch it.
>
> The woman who lived in the cottage was a widow. She lived with her middle-aged daughter. I shared a bedroom with my sister. They were both very kind to us. In fact, we had a wonderful time while we were in Devon. We had complete free rein to go anywhere we liked and do whatever we liked. And while we were there, I don't think we had to bother about the blackout – we were far out in the country and of no interest to German bombers.

We were the only evacuee children in the school. We became very friendly with a family of farmers, the Blights, whose farm was just outside the village. They had a daughter called Amy and she was in the same class as me and she and I became very good friends. But Amy had a teenage brother called Nelson and once he showed me a rabbit, which I thought looked very sweet and I stroked it. But then he made me watch as he pulled its neck to kill it. I'll never forget that. In the end, I think we were rather upset when, without warning, my parents appeared at the front door and told us that they had come to take us home.

STORIES FROM HOST FAMILIES

So much for the experiences of evacuee children. What of the very different experiences of the host families who were compelled to accommodate evacuee children, whether they liked it or not?

Audrey Swindells' mother was very much opposed to the idea. Audrey was 11 and she and her family had just moved to Felixstowe in Suffolk:

> It was announced at school that evacuees were coming to Felixstowe from London and would we please ask our parents if we could take one or two. I asked my mother this question, thinking the answer would be an obvious 'Yes'. However, my mother had heard that they would be coming from the East End of London and, to my astonishment and embarrassment, her answer was categorically, 'No'. I remember that very clearly. I then tried to persuade her because the teacher had made it clear that we should cooperate. 'I'm not having those guttersnipes in my house,' Mummy insisted.

Diana England's mother also had a lucky escape from being overrun by evacuees or billeted soldiers. She and her husband lived in a large eight-bedroom house in rural Berkshire:

> At home we had three maids and a chauffeur. When war was declared, the three maids came to my mother and said that they must leave her to do war work. My mother calmly replied, 'Yes, of course you must. But we are having to have a number of officers billeted on us or perhaps several evacuee children and you would be doing important war work looking after them.' As a result, they all stayed.

Perhaps not surprisingly, neither the officers nor the evacuee children ever arrived.

From the outset, urban children meeting rural families was often a shock to both parties. Tales abounded from the host families of evacuee children being scared half to death by a herd of cows, or verminous, bed-wetting, inner-city children spreading bad urban habits and head lice to the rural children they sat next to in school.

In many ways, evacuation encapsulated two culture clashes, between urban and rural, of course, but also, in many cases, working class and middle class. One organiser had the tricky job of finding homes in rural Bedfordshire for hundreds of East End children. Most of these evacuees were from dockland slums and this gave her all sorts of problems:

All 'my' children were settled in their billets within an hour and a half of their arrival. Then the trouble began. Many housewives undressed their visitors in an outhouse, gave them a scrub, put them to bed and then *burnt* their clothes and sent SOS messages to the WVS representative for clean clothes. Luckily, a car-load arrived late that night and was sent to the cottages early next day. The District Nurse set up a clinic and it took her three weeks to get every child free from 'creatures'.

The national newspapers tried hard to put a positive spin on the subject of the first wave of mass evacuation. A few days later, when things had all died down a bit, the *Daily Mirror* published two reassuring letters from host families. The first said simply, 'There's room in my heart for a hundred children and I'd squeeze them all into my house too, if I could.' Another reader wrote, 'What are a few finger marks on the paintwork beside saving these poor kiddies from the horror of war?' Public opinion was apparently, at this early stage, all for evacuation.

In fact, almost half of this first wave of evacuees had returned home by January 1940, four months after the declaration of war, although the government actively campaigned to stop this return. They had gone back to supposedly dangerous cities but for the next nine months or so they were perfectly safe there.

The second wave of evacuation was in the late summer and autumn of 1940, when the bombing of London began in September. Overall, 827,000 schoolchildren, 524,000 mothers with children under 5 and 12,000 pregnant women were evacuated and, in addition, over 2 million children were 'privately' evacuated to friends and relatives all over the country and, in some cases, abroad. A third wave of evacuation started when V1 and V2 bombs started falling on London.

Lorna Green and her family, like **Audrey Swindells**, experienced the very early wave of evacuation from the point of view of a host family. She lived in a small village in west Somerset. At the end of August 1939, she and her mother:

> Went into Minehead to buy blackout material for curtains. On our return, we found a note that had been slipped under our door. It was from the billeting officer to inform my mother that she should expect to receive five pregnant women. Five! In one rather small spare room. We never knew how the allocation was decided and like most people in the village, bitterly resented the fact that the vicar and his wife, with only one little girl, had no evacuees at all. We were just told that the vicar's wife was delicate.
>
> Anyway, we waited for them in the village hall, where tea and biscuits were ready. Pregnant women, mothers and babies, toddlers and bewildered, labelled children. Eventually, they were all sorted out and a compromise was reached regarding the pregnant women. They went elsewhere and we were to receive a mother and baby. And as it turned out, Mrs Skiddamore and her baby were delightful and at her request, her sister and her gentle, small boy joined her.

The allocation of city children to rural families was a logistical nightmare in some cases. One commentator described it thus, 'There were scenes reminiscent of a cross between an early Roman slave market and Selfridges bargain basement.' Selection was done on a 'pick-your-own' system with host families inevitably choosing children who looked the cleanest and best dressed. Sickly, smelly or grubby children were left to the last.

★ ★ ★

So how did the evacuees fit into village life? Badly, it seems in some cases. **Lorna Green** continued:

> Most of them were homesick for London and didn't fit in with the village culture. They went to the Butcher's Arms pub in the evening – where else could they go? But village women did not frequent the pub.

These remarks paralleled those of young mothers from big cities finding themselves marooned in rural villages. For the most part, they were bored witless with nowhere to go and nothing to do. There were numerous stories of young women who complained that there was a limit to the number of times you could push a pram around the village green, however picturesque it might be. Where were the noise, shops, cinemas, street markets and bustle of the cities? One young mother from Bow in east London summed it up, 'I'd rather die in my own house than stay here and die of boredom.'

Lorna summed up the cultural differences between evacuees from London and the people in her Somerset village:

> This alien behaviour (going to the pub), as well as indulgence in make-up ('and they don't wash it off before they go to bed!') led to the attitude that many of them were 'no better than they should be'.

Eleanor Frost, the day after war was declared, wrote:

> Went to the First Air lecture in Clifton at 8.30. Returned at 9.30 wondering why Edith and Mother had not followed me there. I found that they had been met by a party of people who were asking for our house. An evacuee mother from Bow in east London with four little boys all under seven had to be taken in. The man who brought them to us was very good.

These unexpected evacuees then moved into the servants' quarters on the top floor of her large house and **Eleanor** left it to her servants to look after them.

Occasionally she referred to them. On 4 October she wrote, 'They sound like a nestful of twittering birds up there at the top of our house.' The next day, she wrote:

> Mrs Barrett took them all out for the day. The mother said to her, 'If it hadn't been for the war I'd never have been in such a posh house as this!' When the children returned I decided to let them play in the garden where they tumbled about like puppies … The four of them cling as close as four needles to a magnet.

Later **Eleanor** recorded, 'I hear that the kitchen is indescribable at meal times! And the children's mother is surprised that we are always down by 8.30 – she supposed that people like us should not come down before mid-day!'

Enid Beebee, living in Redruth in Cornwall, also experienced evacuation in the other direction:

Early on in the war, the local Boys' Grammar School in Redruth had to take in all the boys who'd been evacuated from St Marylebone Grammar School in London. There wasn't really enough room for them but somehow the school had to find makeshift classrooms all over the town, in unlikely places like pubs, chapels, barns, sheds, garages and shops.

At home we also had to take in an evacuee from London. His name was Alan Hickman. He was very nice but it meant we were very crowded in our house when he arrived. But we didn't have any say in the matter – we were just told we had to have him.

My parents had one bedroom and Alan another, so my sister and I had to sleep downstairs on two chairs that folded out and were made into beds. They weren't very comfortable!

Hazel Bray was now doing her first teaching job in south Devon and this involved teaching many evacuees:

I started to teach at the Elementary School in Buckfastleigh. I had a class of fifty-two infants! Many of them were evacuee children from the East End of London. Obviously they missed their parents terribly, so it was a difficult start to my teaching career. I remember that the classes were so big there weren't nearly enough exercise books to go round so we had to give out rolls of old wallpaper for the children to write and draw on.

Joan Fell had a similar perspective on evacuation:

My parents had two small boys living with them, both of them called David. They were evacuees from the East End of London. They became quite fond of those boys and they were probably better fed and better clothed than they were back home. But when their parents came down from London to see how they were getting on, they insisted on taking them back home, I suppose because they were afraid of losing them.

★ ★ ★

For a different perspective on the evacuation of children, it is estimated that approximately 38,000 evacuees were abandoned by their parents, or at least left 'unclaimed', by the end of the war.

The government, with the help of an army of civil servants, really had done an incredible job preparing the country for the expected Blitz. They had distributed gas masks to every adult and child, provided Anderson shelters, or alternatively Morrison shelters, to almost every family and prepared and then enforced the blackout. And as if that wasn't enough, they had evacuated over 1.5 million children and young mothers away from urban 'target' areas to the relative safety of rural England. Now they were to discover whether or not those precautionary measures would be enough.

4

Blitzed

The Bristol Blitz

The word 'blitz' was first used by the British popular press in 1940, although it's questionable why they chose the German word for 'lightning' in this context. Whatever you call it, it was a sustained aerial bombing campaign aimed at most of Britain's industrial cities, ports and railways.

Over 52,000 civilians were killed during this bombing campaign and many more were injured. Almost half of these casualties were in the capital, where more than 1 million houses were destroyed or badly damaged. But significantly, this war was unlike any war before. Why? Because there were a huge number of households in Britain, the so-called 'Home Front', where women and their children saw as much action, endured much more hardship and experienced as much danger as their husbands, boyfriends and brothers in the armed services. These were the women who were bombed, again and again.

When it came to experiencing a blitz, Bristol was one of the first cities to be bombed and then it came in for more than its fair share. Between June 1940 and May 1944, Bristol was the fourth most-bombed city in the country, behind only London, Liverpool and Birmingham. Because the two diarists, **HJF** and **Eleanor Frost**, as well as a number of the women interviewed for this book, were from Bristol, the focus in this chapter is mainly on the experiences of women during the Blitz on that city.

The start of the bombing campaign on Bristol was announced on German radio on 24 June 1940, two-and-a-half months before the beginning of the London Blitz:

Bristol, one of the greatest English trading and free cities has been bombed. The revenge of the German Air Force for England's sly night piracy has begun. German forbearance is exhausted. The time for settlement has come.

Before long, the frequent wailing of air-raid sirens was having such a depressing effect on the civilian population that questions were asked in the Commons. One MP remarked:

I have received a large number of letters, especially from women, saying that the sound of these sirens has a much more depressing effect upon them than the bombs, and is he aware that what the country wants is a trumpet call of challenge and not the wailing of the damned?

The government minister concerned ignored this request.

To begin with, the bombing raids on Bristol were often in daylight when a lot of people were away from home, shopping or at work. On 2 July 1940, **HJF** wrote, 'The siren went just as I was leaving work and I had to go down to the shelter there, in the garden, until the All Clear':

3 July: To the Embassy Picture House at 5 p.m. and the siren sounded at 5.25. The manager informed the audience that they could leave the building if they wished, but that the show would continue. Home at 8.15.

19 July: When out this afternoon, Jean and I were caught in air raid that lasted from 3.30 to 5.15. We were in Messrs Bakers' basement shelter, where it became so hot that several of the girl assistants became faint and had to be given water. I do wish the wardens would let one go home. I feel most unsafe and unhappy in a crowded cellar and would rather die in the open air.

These early raids were also described by **Eleanor Frost**:

4 July 1940: German bombers have just gone over with great gun bursts making a welcome din. They were followed, I think, by our fighters. Mother and I sat under the stairs – once the guns begin there is no time to get to the dug-out. One is so unused to being awakened suddenly by such a racket – the peculiarly distressing wail of the sirens and the terrific explosion of guns or both together. I felt sick and faint.

5 July: Mother, Edith and I now sleep on camp beds in the dug-out so when we hear the warning all we have to do is shut the steel door. We have brought our stirrup pump down to the ground floor and put it next to buckets of water in the lobby and we also have buckets of water on every floor.

6 July: This morning the first raid came as we were dressing so we all went to the dug-out. After they had passed out of sight we returned and finished dressing. Then in the middle of breakfast back they came so we seized our plates and sat on the cellar stairs and continued our meal.

Soon after that, **Eleanor** noted one result of these frequent bombing raids:

It is extraordinary how the children of the elementary school play at sirens and taking cover. One hears them give excellent imitations of the sirens then dash away and hide.

Yesterday I heard some children dawdling and chattering on their way home from school and then suddenly the sirens went and they all tore away up the road as fast as their little legs could carry them. Such a sudden cessation of chatter followed by such a patter of small feet.

On 11 July 1940 she described two practical things she could do in response to the bombing:

We are all now wearing identity discs with our names engraved upon them. They are fine silver chains with a small disc and are very smart. And today we have taken all our old Georgian silver to the Bank, also Mother's rings to be stored till the war is over.

16 July: Today good Mrs Labercombe arrived for her weekly day of work here. She told me what she did when the warning of an air raid sounded. 'When we hear the sirens we rush down to the shelter and the first thing we does is have a good laugh – there's Violet with her old slacks and me in me winter knickers. What a sight!' I thought this was truly the female counterpart of the cheerful Tommy in the trenches.

HJF is far less cheerful than Mrs Labercombe:

23 July: Six Air Raid warnings! I have had a very bad liver attack. Think I caught a chill running up and down the stairs three times in the night. Feel very ill tonight. Doctor says that I am suffering from nervous debility and gave me a prescription for a bottle of medicine. But in my heart I just know I am very tired and really need a rest.

Soon after that, **HJF** contrived to make the experience slightly less miserable, 'This afternoon I bought two "siren" suits of warm wool for Jean and me as we don't like to rush down to the basement at night in nightdresses and dressing gowns.' A siren suit is a loose-fitting one-piece garment, a bit like overalls. They became identified with Winston Churchill, who regularly wore them, even when meeting other world leaders. They fastened at the front and many also had a craftily inserted flap at the back, which was easily opened to allow the wearer, usually a woman, to use a toilet without having to remove the entire suit.

24 July: Germans lost 12 planes today. [In fact **HJF** was mistaken. No German aircraft were shot down at all.]

28 July: Out in car to Clevedon and had lunch (cold fowl) and sandwiches under the trees in the car park. We then sat in deckchairs by the swimming pool. [It seems it was still possible to live a relatively normal life even when bombs were falling most nights.]

15 October: Heavy gun-fire throughout the evening and right into the night. We are living on our nerves.

25 October: Heavy firing at midnight. There is a rumour that Lord Haw-Haw said in his broadcast last night that German planes will be bombing Bristol.

It's worth recording here that the heavy gunfire **HJF** referred to was generally ineffective. Only three German aircraft were actually shot down over the entire Bristol area during the course of the war and in some raids, many more people were killed by falling shells from our own guns than from German bombs.

It's interesting that the broadcasts of Lord Haw-Haw were at least half-believed and that **HJF** openly admitted that she listened to them. **Ruby Spragg** also admitted to listening to these broadcasts but then added, 'My father became so angry when he heard that voice announcing "Germany call-ing, Germany calling" that he used to shout at the radio and once threw a boot at it. It missed!'

Lord Haw-Haw was the name given to William Joyce, who was an American citizen, born in Brooklyn, New York in 1906. His family moved to Ireland when he was 3 – his father was Irish–American – and then to England when he was 17. There, he became a supporter of Oswald Mosely and his British Union of Fascists then later the British National Socialist Party. Joyce subsequently travelled to Germany just before he could be arrested. From there he broadcast propaganda from September 1939 to April 1945, always beginning, 'Germany calling, Germany calling', spoken with an affected upper-class English accent, perhaps to give what he said more credence. He was eventually captured by British forces and hanged for treason on 3 January 1946 in Wandsworth Prison, despite the fact that he was an American citizen and a naturalised German.

★ ★ ★

The frequency of air raids was affected by weather conditions. On 30 October, **HJF** wrote, 'Air raids have lessened considerably. Very wet and windy tonight and I think we shall have a quiet night as it is too rough "upstairs" for Jerry.'

On 8 November, she wrote, 'Newspapers announce that Mr Chamberlain is gravely ill. Being a peace-loving man no doubt the bombing of this country and all its attendant horrors is breaking his heart.' Mr Chamberlain had, in fact, been diagnosed with terminal bowel cancer in July 1940. He left London for the last time on 9 September and died on 9 November 1941, aged 71.

Lorna Green, by now a medical student in Bristol, wrote in her memoirs about her experiences of being bombed:

All too soon the Bristol Blitz really started. A bomb demolished the front garden of a neighbouring house, our kitchen window was broken and the floor covered with glass. This was in spite of the sticky tape which was put across the glass to prevent shattering. I found all this extremely exhilarating and hated to miss a raid. At the time I was ashamed of this adrenaline-induced thrill and never mentioned it.

In the autumn of 1940 part of the university, including the Anatomy Department, was bombed. A number of half-dissected corpses were destroyed and as a result my knowledge of anatomy never reached below the knee – the lower leg and foot were no more.

The raids on Bristol continued with varying degrees of destruction. But they were nothing compared to the raid of 24/25 November 1940. The German High Command described it as their first really big attack on '*Bruder*', their code name for Bristol which ironically meant 'brother' in English. The raid resulted in the mass destruction of the centre of Bristol, the deaths of 207 Bristolians and injuries to a further 689 with 10,000 homes damaged and 14,000 people made homeless. Although heavy, casualties were however far lighter than they might have been because it was a Sunday and there were fewer people at work or shopping in the city centre.

On 25 November, **HJF** wrote:

A very terrible raid on Bristol. Commenced at 6.30 last night and ended at about midnight. The telephone rang in the middle of the raid and as Daddy was absent on fire duty I crept up and answered the call. It was the Head Warden of a hostel who asked me to call upon a neighbour who was not on the phone and ask him why he had not reported to work. I found my way to the man's house by the lights from the guns and searchlights and after some difficulty made him hear for he was with his family in the basement. He said it was unsafe to leave his wife and children during the raid apart from the danger to himself from falling shrapnel but that he would report in as soon as things 'upstairs' were quiet.

Joan Watkins also described that raid in considerable detail, despite the time lapse of over seventy years:

I was 13 and living in north Bristol at the time. On the evening of 24 November, I'd been having tea with my Aunt Dorothy who lived about a mile away. At 6.45 p.m. the air-raid sirens started and my aunt didn't know whether to send me home as quickly as possible or keep me with her. I persuaded her that if I ran most of the way I could be home safely in less than a quarter of an hour.

Anyway, I started running and when I was nearly home all hell was let loose. There was loud gunfire from every direction, bombs falling and shrapnel coming down from out of the sky. I was desperate to keep going because I definitely didn't want to go into the big communal air-raid shelter at the end of our road – I never liked going in there because it smelt of wee. So I tried hard to make myself invisible to the air-raid wardens but one of them collared me and said, 'You're coming into this shelter, whether you like it or not. It's far too dangerous out here.' So, very reluctantly, I had to spend the next six hours in that shelter, which was packed with people, many of whom had been on their way home from church when the raid started.

During that time, the noise of the bombs exploding and the guns firing was tremendous. There were some hysterical ladies, I remember, who were convinced they were going to die and a girl near me started sobbing very loudly. But I remember thinking that she only did it so that her sailor boyfriend had an excuse to put his arm around her. Strangely enough, I felt no fear at all and I certainly didn't think *I* was going to die.

Nobody spoke to me the whole time I was there, from 7 in the evening till 1 in the morning, and I think I was bored for most of the time, which seems difficult to believe now. Eventually, when the all-clear sounded, we were able to look outside. The whole sky was red from the fires down in the city centre, with what was left of the tall buildings silhouetted against the skyline. In fact, it looked as though the whole world was on fire.

After that, I ran the rest of the way home and when I got there my parents were out in the road waiting for me and talking to all our neighbours – that's what seemed to happen after a raid, people congregated in the street and talked about what had happened and how much destruction there'd been. I remember that my mother pretended to be very cross because I'd been out for so long but I think in fact that she was terribly relieved that I was home safely – and alive. Eventually, we all went off to bed.

The next day will always stick in my mind. Then I saw for myself the destruction that the raid had caused. It was a Monday, so I tried to go to school as though nothing had happened. My school was built on the ruins of the old Bristol Castle, right in the centre of the city.

Anyway, I set out but at the bus stop a woman told me that there were no buses running that day so I had to walk. As I got nearer the city centre, I was met by scenes of absolute and utter devastation. Whole streets had collapsed into rubble and there were hose pipes and water everywhere. But I desperately wanted to keep going, to find out how bad it would be a little further on. And if I was careful and no one noticed me, then I'd be able to see much more.

So I hopped over the hose pipes which seemed to be curling everywhere and tried to stay in the middle of the road where there were only a few bricks or lumps of fallen masonry. Anyway, I just kept on going. There were piles of rubble everywhere – and still nobody noticed me!

Eventually, I got to a big shop I knew well and I realised with horror that there was nothing left of it except for piles of rubble and smoke and steam and clothes models lying in disarray, with no clothes on. There were still firemen working there and I was sure I was going to be seen and told to go back. But I was determined to just look round the corner to Castle Street where my school was.

When I finally got there, Castle Street was no more. Only one wall of my school was still standing – just. Everything else was just rubble and ruin. I stood and stared in disbelief until a fireman saw me, a 13-year-old girl in her school uniform, standing in the middle of this total devastation. He let out a stream of very rude words, some of which I'd never heard before, but their meaning was clear – 'What are you doing here? Go home!' But by then I'd seen enough – I had no school to go to. So I turned tail and ran, as fast as my legs would carry me.

Rubble and ruin in Castle Street, very near to **Joan Watkins'** school. (© David Facey. Facey Collection. Bristol Archives: 41969/1/12)

HJF also recorded her very personal feelings in the aftermath of that raid:

26 November: Poor Bristol! Our museum is gone and many other places are smouldering ruins. We have no water and Daddy and I seem to be suffering from slight shock as neither of us want to eat but each of us has a great thirst.

The next month brought no let-up. On 1 December, **HJF** wrote:

Victoria Street is a shambles and fires from burnt buildings are still smouldering. But there is still a spark of humour flashing in these terrible times. One shopkeeper, with all his windows blown out, has chalked up, 'No window cleaners required'. Another had 'Glasgow was once in Scotland. Now we have glass go here.' And another, 'Blasted but not busted.'

Eleanor Frost also wrote about this raid:

At 6.30 p.m. an intensive and fierce bombardment of Bristol began and lasted until 1.30 a.m. We all sat in the refuge room but it was a nerve-racking experience. With the constant whistle and crash of exploding bombs. Edith and I sat on either side of Mother and at one point Edith held her hands for it seemed impossible that we should not be hit. The next morning I felt as though this would be almost more than I could bear. Mother looked what I felt.

On 3 December, **HJF** wrote:

Another heavy raid on Bristol last night. Bristol is certainly broken. No water, gas, or electricity. The windows in our house are blown out and we have to wear our winter coats all day in the house. We have no facilities for making a cup of tea, as the all-electric house of which I was so proud is useless with no current. There is besides no water.

7 December: Being still without water and electric light I lit a fire in the kitchen grate and made a cup of tea with water that Daddy obtained from a hydrant. I commenced to make the fire at 8 a.m. and only had the tea ready to drink at 9.45. How did our grandmothers get their men folks' breakfasts ready in time for them to go to their morning work?

Ruby Spragg lived in the centre of Bristol, near Temple Meads station:

I was 17 when the bombing started. We didn't have a shelter in our backyard, it wasn't big enough. So instead, we just used to shelter under the
stairs where we kept the coal.

The bombs often came very near and we almost got used to having our
windows broken by bomb-blast and having to sweep up broken glass the
next morning. In fact, some windows were broken so often we just boarded
them up. But when the bombing got really bad we used to go into a neighbour's Anderson shelter and in there we used to feel the thud of the impact.
It went right through you.

One of our neighbours was actually killed by the blast from a bomb. She
didn't look as though she'd been hurt at all but in fact she was dead.

Sheila Kellard also lived near the centre of Bristol:

We had a small brick shelter in our back garden at 21 Maxse Road, but it
was on the surface because my mother suffered from claustrophobia. In
there, I always wore my siren suit which was made of an itchy serge material. I also took my koala bear with me – funnily enough, I've still got it!

I used to go out to our shelter every evening at about 6 o'clock and I had
my supper there, something simple like a cheese sandwich and some ginger
beer in a stone jar. I also took lots of books with me and used to sit up in
bed and read by the light of a Tilley lamp. My parents came to join me at
about 9.45 and then we all tried to get some sleep. Some nights that was
very difficult. And sometimes I had to go to our outside loo and that could
be very frightening if it was in the middle of a big raid.

Some of the women I spoke to remembered some individual raids. One woman
recalled, for example, that, at 11.45 a.m. on 25 September 1940, fifty-eight
Heinkel 111 bombers flew in low over the suburbs of west Bristol. Three minutes later, they attacked the Bristol Aeroplane Company. In total, 350 bombs
were dropped on the factory buildings, causing a huge amount of destruction.

But far more destructive were bombs which dropped on the communal
air-raid shelters, just outside the factory buildings. The raid was all over in
less than a minute.

One woman working at the factory remembered hearing the tune of
'Marching Through Georgia' over the tannoy, the signal for the workers

to take cover. It had happened many times before, so nobody was unduly alarmed. But on this occasion, seventy-two people were killed and 166 injured. Nineteen later died of their injuries. Immediately outside the factory perimeter, another fifty-eight people were killed and 159 injured. It was later reported that an army NCO marching a squad towards the factory would not allow his men to break ranks to take cover. They were all killed.

The death toll was so high because a stick of high-explosive bombs fell on six crowded air-raid shelters. The scenes confronting the rescue parties were horrific. Some of the shelters had caved in, burying the occupants. Others had been blasted wide open, mutilating the occupants beyond recognition. The task of identification was impossible. Rescue work was temporarily halted at 12.16 p.m. when another air-raid siren sounded. But this time it was triggered by only one high-flying German aircraft taking photographs of the after-effects of what had been, for them, a highly successful raid.

One woman, Alice Peacock, was with a group of friends in No. 1 Shelter, chatting and knitting, when a bomb exploded right on top of their shelter. Two hours later, she was pulled out of the rubble, still alive but only just. Later in hospital, both her legs had to be amputated. Six months later, with two artificial limbs fitted, she went back to work at the same aeroplane factory.

The same afternoon one woman reported:

All the other employees at Filton were sent home because of the tragedy. They arrived home white and shaken, none of them being able to coherently tell the story of what happened and wondering how their friends and workmates could ever be properly buried. The shelters at Filton were never re-opened but were sealed over and became a tomb.

Barbara Steadman said this about the raid on Filton:

My mother was actually working in the factory that morning and she told me about the panic as the bombs were exploding in the factory – it was so bad the men trampled over the women in their desperation to get out and get into the shelters. You never read about that in the papers, do you?

Ruby Spragg also clearly remembered that raid:

I knew a boy who was working at that factory in Filton, he lived opposite us. He told me how he saw with his own eyes several of the people he worked with killed by the German bombs. Many of them were his friends and it affected him deeply. He was never the same after that.

Out of Danger

During the bombing raids on Bristol and many other cities, the so-called 'Blitz spirit' was sorely tested and many people found ways of getting away from the bombing using whatever form of transport they could find. Most just stayed away overnight, others escaped from danger for much longer.

It became common for whole families to hitch a lift on a lorry and pay the driver to take them to a lay-by or quiet lane outside the city. There they could spend the night, asleep in the back of the lorry, uncomfortable but relatively safe. If the driver didn't agree to park up for the night, those families used to sleep in barns, woods, hedgerows or even open fields. Others used to get together and hire a coach to take them to a village hall where they could sleep on the floor.

This mass exodus of families out of the big cities caused a lot of bad feeling among those who stayed. As one Bristol resident put it:

> People going out to the countryside were a sore point. They left others to do the fire watching and our attitude was 'Let their bloody houses burn'. There was a lot of ill-feeling. We didn't agree with it, the ones with cars who made their way each night to the safety of the countryside leaving us to fight fires in the streets where they lived. We were really angry with them.

Audrey Swindells confirmed that this was also true in Birmingham:

> My Uncle George was an air-raid warden and he said that anyone who left their home for the safety of the countryside was supposed to leave a key with the warden. Then one night, an incendiary got stuck on the roof of one particular empty house. The front door was a beautifully carved, solid oak door and he had to take a hatchet and chop into it, enter, go upstairs and put out the fire on the roof with a stirrup pump. Then, of course, he had to barricade the doorway. And all because the stupid people who owned the house didn't leave a key somewhere.

Portsmouth was also very badly bombed and **Suzanne Best** described how she escaped to safety:

> When the bombing was really bad, I used to go with my mother and my brother and sister out of the centre of Portsmouth to the quieter and much safer suburb of Waterlooville, nearly 5 miles away. We usually walked and I used to carry my nightclothes, my toothbrush, a sponge and a flannel in a small suitcase. My father remained at home because he was an air-raid warden. There in Waterlooville, we stayed with family friends and I slept on a blow-up mattress.

Other people stayed away for longer than one night. On 8 December 1940, **HJF** wrote:

> Out in the car in afternoon to Burrington Combe about 15 miles from Bristol. We saw a large colony of caravans occupied by people who have fled from the city. Apparently cottagers and farmers are besieged by people wanting accommodation. Many people sleep in their cars along the combe and at the side of the road, with tarpaulins and tents. Washing hangs on lines tied to the rocks, and cooking pots and children are scattered around. The colony reminds me of a refugee camp.

The authorities were concerned about this nightly exodus and started a 'Stay Put' campaign, which included threats to billet homeless families in houses left empty. This worked, up to a point, but it's estimated that at the height of the Blitz as many as 10,000 people left Bristol every night.

Some people, usually those with money, chose to stay in hotels away from the city where the bombs were falling. **HJF** was one of them:

> 17 August: Jean and I left Bristol by car at 11 a.m. for a short stay at Clevedon. Daddy unable to come. Arrived at the Oaklands Hotel in time for lunch.

> 18 August: Slept well all night — my first good night for a long time. This afternoon listened to the Silver Band on the Prom. Wrote to Daddy who has stayed back in Bristol.

21 August: Another lovely night. Siren went about noon but we neither saw nor heard anything else. Daddy reports that houses at Filton down like a pack of cards in the last bombing raid.

Eventually **HJF** joined the ranks of those who left their houses in central Bristol to take refuge more permanently in the country outside:

26 January 1941: Redhill farmer rang us up to ask if we would like to take two rooms in his cottage, for night refuge, at 25/- a week. I agreed.

27 January: Out to see rooms at Redhill. But we have come across a snag – we cannot leave our Bristol home without a fire watcher on the premises. Also, there is a general feeling of animosity towards those who leave their houses as soon as the sirens go, thus leaving it to the residents who remain to attend to them. The matter is left until Saturday for decision.

28 January: Out to Redhill and paid £5 for two rooms for one month. Back in town bought blankets and flannelette sheets (£7 4s 11d) for the beds at the cottage.

Three months later, however, they were back in their house in Bristol. The bombing was still bad:

20 March: Over to see the mater [her mother-in-law perhaps?]. She will not go to bed as the house is now open with only broken glass in the windows and the Venetian blinds blown away from their fittings. She is afraid of being murdered in her sleep, poor darling!

Eleanor Frost had this to say about getting away from the bombing, except that in her case her 'escape' was for far longer:

2 December 1940: The raid last night was so bad we have decided to throw ourselves on Phylis's mercy for the weekend. [It is not clear who Phylis was. An old friend or member of the Frost family perhaps?]

Eleanor and her immediate family left Bristol by car that day, to drive to Wigley, near Ludlow:

As the afternoon shortened into dusk I felt as though we were fleeing from a horror and then, at last, we were in Wigley and as we sat in the warm study drinking sherry with no sound outside but the gentle sighing of the wind in the trees it felt like another world, a haven of almost unbelievably quiet happiness. I shall never forget the quiet of that night and the lamp-lit, fire-lit bedroom. It was the most extreme contrast to the night before.

It wasn't until over a year later that **Eleanor** at last returned to Bristol:

8 January 1942: Mother and I returned to Hill Side, Bristol. Not an easy thing to do. I found the return after an absence of 13 months extremely difficult and found the old sensations of nervous sickness at black-out. This lasted about 2 to 3 weeks. I can understand that if an airman crashes and is not hurt it is essential for him to go up again at once or else it may become impossible for him to fly again.

Clearly then, if you were wealthy enough and had a car and relatives or friends in the country it was perfectly possible to get out of the big cities where the bombs were dropping. The Blitz was, for many people, a tale of extreme stress, real danger and terrible fear. But for a lucky few, it was also a time when they could get away and out of danger. The Blitz spirit really did have its limits.

THE LONDON BLITZ

The London Blitz was far worse than the attacks on Bristol, although it didn't begin until late in the afternoon of 7 September 1940. It went on and on, whatever the weather, with only one night's break, for fifty-six out of the following fifty-seven days and nights and was far more intense and destructive than anything Bristol experienced.

On 8 September, **HJF** wrote, 'London was heavily bombed last night. 400 reported dead and 1,400 injured.' In fact, 348 bombers took part in that first day and night raid. They dropped 300 tons of high-explosive bombs and many thousands of incendiaries onto the London Docks and densely populated East End. The raid lasted until 4.30 a.m. the next morning. Unfortunately, the water mains were badly damaged and it was low tide in the Thames, so the firemen's hoses literally ran dry. Tea and sugar stored in dockside warehouses caught fire and gave off a sickly stench, boiling paint shot up into the sky, buildings collapsed, the intense heat blistered paintwork on boats moored in the Thames and the air was so full of burning debris and sparks that it hurt to breathe.

On 13 September, **HJF** wrote, 'The 6 o'clock news says that a bomb has damaged Buckingham Palace.' Five bombs were dropped by one German raider. The king and queen were unharmed and were said to be drinking tea at the time. The queen later remarked, 'I am glad we have been bombed. It makes me feel I can look the East End in the eye.'

HJF recorded on 16 September, '185 German war machines destroyed in a fight over Britain.' The true figure was fifty-six German aircraft shot down, while the RAF lost twenty-seven. Truth, as always, was the first casualty of war.

Eve Cherry was living in London at that time:

I remember the first big raid. I was looking out of an upstairs window at the sight of London burning. It was absolutely terrible.

I was living with my mother in the flat over the shop she owned. The two of us used to shelter in the room in the middle of the house and hope for the best. It was the safest place to be and we put our camp beds in there.

Then one night a big bomb fell two or three houses away and the blast almost blew the top floor of our house off. Soon after that, an air-raid warden warned me on no account to go up to the top of the house because it was so unstable. But the thing that concerned me most was our cat, Whisky. I eventually found him cowering under an armchair upstairs, covered in plaster dust but otherwise unharmed.

Another warden came to examine the extent of the damage. It was so unstable he was able to push out the upstairs walls with one hand!

I also remember that a shop in the same street as ours, a grocer's, suffered a near miss and the contents of the shop were blown all over the road. There was jam, marmalade, sugar and various groceries everywhere.

Although the docks and the East End were by far the worst hit areas of London, the West End was also sometimes targeted and during one raid, the Café de Paris in Piccadilly was hit. It advertised itself as the 'safest and gayest restaurant in town' because it was 20ft below ground. One evening, a popular band leader named Ken 'Snake Hips' Johnson was conducting a number called 'Oh Johnny, Oh Johnny. How you can love?' when a bomb came down an air shaft and exploded on the dance floor. A contemporary newspaper reported:

Debris was hurled in all directions ... The dancers hurled to the floor by the blast were lying everywhere – some dead, including Johnson himself and the cafe's head waiter, and many more injured. What had been a night-club became a nightmare. Heaps of wreckage crushed heaps of dead and maimed, a shamble of silver slippers, broken magnums, torn sheet music, and dented saxophones.

Another report described how the place was packed with:

young officers and their elegant girlfriends in evening dresses, sipping champagne and cocktails. Minutes later some of the young officers were carrying out their dead girlfriends while others were desperately tearing up the dresses the girls were wearing to make bandages.

During the Blitz, many Londoners in both the East End and West End felt much safer on the platform of an underground station than in a jerry-built terrace house or an Anderson shelter. Every night, over 150,000 would buy a ticket or simply vault the barrier and go as deep as possible down into the underground system. Touts or spivs offered their services to reserve a pitch on a desperately crowded station platform for half a crown.

Sleeping on concrete with no sanitation was extremely uncomfortable but at least it was relatively safe. The government wisely soon gave up trying to ban the use of the underground as a giant public air-raid shelter and even opened up three disused stations to alleviate the overcrowding. This over-crowding was helped a little when people took to sleeping sideways on every step of the escalators, both up and down. After 10.30 p.m., the electricity supply was switched off, which meant that the tunnels could be used as public toilets, albeit foul-smelling and unsanitary.

Rose Jennings wasn't living near an underground station. She lived in Belvedere, north Kent. She remembered:

German bombers used to come over every night. At about 6 o'clock the siren went and we could hear them, and sometimes see them overhead, wave after wave of them. They were on their way to bomb the London Docks. I sheltered in the cellar of our house at first, but I soon got fed up with that and took refuge under the stairs instead – it was much more comfortable although probably not so safe. Anyway, we used to hear the whistle of the bombs as they were falling and I remember very clearly that as the whistling noise got louder and louder, I thought that perhaps I only had a few seconds left to live.

She later described what eventually happened to her family home:

An enormous land mine exploded in the garden of our house and tore off the roof and part of the back wall. My mother was trapped in the cellar for six hours until air-raid wardens eventually came to dig her out. We had to put an enormous canvas over what was left of the building to try and keep the rain out but we couldn't live there any longer.

Some gypsies were employed to make the house safe before it could be rebuilt. They found an old trunk in the attic of our house with lots of flags in. They decorated our house with those flags. It was a cheerful, defiant gesture.

Rosemary Strydom was also living in London, in Pimlico:

We were in the thick of it, living so close to Victoria station, which was a frequent target for German bombs. I remember we used to shelter in a coal hole underneath the pavement outside our house which we reached by climbing down some iron steps. We cleaned it up and made it reasonably comfortable, although we never had electric lights down there, only candles.

Vera Bartlett was also in London during the Blitz. She was living on her own with two young children to look after while her husband Ted was away fighting:

When there was an air raid I had to wake the children and take them down into the cellar. After that, it was the noisiness of the Blitz that I remember most clearly, what with the whistle of the bombs coming down, then the huge crash when they exploded, the ack-ack guns firing all at the same time and the sound of the German bombers overhead – a horrible jerky sound it was.

A woman on the top flat used to have hysterics during the raids and I was very worried that her screaming would frighten the children, so I had to get away from her as much as possible. Looking back on it now, I think I was too busy with the children to be frightened. I just had to stay calm for their sake, or at least pretend to be calm. I did have a horror, though, of being buried alive and being separated from them. That was my greatest fear – of being separated from my children.

When these bombing raids were going on we used to dread moonlit nights because that was when they were worst. The bombs usually fell in sticks of three, I remember, and when two had dropped you waited a few seconds and wondered whether the last one was going to fall on you.

MONDSCHEINSONATE – THE DESTRUCTION OF COVENTRY

The London Blitz was horrific in its scale of destruction. But the city of Coventry suffered some of the most severe and intense attacks of all.

On 16 November 1940, **HJF** wrote, 'Coventry badly damaged in an air raid on the 14th with over 1,000 casualties. The King visited that city today.'

That raid was probably the most devastating bombing raid of the war so far. In total, 449 German bombers dropped 30,000 incendiaries, 1,600 tons of high-explosive bombs and fifty landmines. Only one bomber was shot down but 568 people were killed and a further 863 badly injured. Ironically, the Luftwaffe code-named the operation *Mondscheinsonate*, or *Moonlight Sonata*, which is a very well-known gentle, peaceful sonata by Beethoven.

The raid was one of the most horrific of the entire Luftwaffe bombing campaign. Contemporary reports included the following facts:

- The job of the German bombers was made much easier by the weather. It was a cloudless, moonlit night.
- The smell and heat of the burning city reached into the cockpits of the German bombers.
- The air stank of burning flesh and bodies, some mutilated beyond recognition.
- A 14-year-old girl, Jean Taylor, making her way to school the next day, reported seeing a dog running down the street with a child's arm in its mouth.
- One man reported being pursued down the street by a knee-high river of boiling butter after one bomb set fire to a dairy.
- Seventy-one factories were damaged which was three-quarters of the total number in the city.
- In the aftermath of the bombing, more than half the city's population fled out into the countryside to stay with friends or relatives or, in some cases, to sleep in fields, despite the winter weather.
- Coventry's mediaeval cathedral, St Michael's, was destroyed.

- Following the raid, Joseph Goebbels came up with a new word, '*Coventrieren*', meaning to raze a city to the ground.

As a symbol of reconciliation after the war, Coventry and Dresden became twinned cities in 1959.

Betty Gough was living in Coventry at this time and she remembered:

It was a night of destruction such as never before. Hitler promised to turn Coventry from a bed of roses into a bed of ashes and he kept his promise.

We didn't hear the air-raid sirens that night – the Jerries were too quick for us. In no time at all, the whistling of bombs, followed by explosions, bangs and crashes filled the air. It was deafening. And then the roof of our house collapsed just as we were diving for cover under the stairs. Soon after that, with the roof gone, we could look up and see searchlights criss-crossing the sky, a red glow from all the fires, billowing smoke and even German aircraft overhead.

I remember my mother held me very, very tightly while I shook with fear. 'Oh God, thank you,' I thought – 'at least we'll die together.'

Then we heard an air-raid warden shouting at us to keep calm. I thought, that's one order I won't be able to obey. Anyway, he then came to get us and take us somewhere safer. I remember how he led my mother and me by the hand, half-running, half-stumbling through the falling shrapnel and bombs and collapsing buildings with the sound of people shouting and screaming all around us, to a public shelter.

We spent the whole night there with more and more people crowding in until there was standing room only. I remember listening to tragic stories of loved ones missing or killed and pets lost. Then some brave soul started singing, 'There'll always be an England' followed by 'Roll out the barrel' and we all joined in, well, some of us ...

The next morning, we emerged to a scene of total devastation. But where was our home? Gone! And everything looked so different. People looked so much older – and stunned. Some were desperately searching for their belongings amid the rubble of their homes while fires were still burning.

So there we were with no water, no food and no home. We had nothing! And I never did find our cat, missing presumed dead.

Then my mother asked God to send help to get us away and God didn't fail us. A distant Welsh relative offered to help us escape from the still burning city of Coventry and we were evacuated to Wales, where we had food, drink, a hot bath and a peaceful night's sleep. We were safe and sound after the most horrific night of my life.

On the night of the bombing of Coventry, **Audrey Swindells** was sheltering with her family in a suburb of Birmingham. Fortunately for them, Birmingham wasn't being bombed that night:

> I remember my father opened the door of our shelter and stepped outside. 'Oh, my God!' he said, 'Nothing's happening here, but some other poor devils are definitely getting it tonight.' My mother went out and so did I.
>
> In the direction we were looking – Coventry was about 20 miles away – the whole sky was flaming red, the searchlights were sweeping the sky, there were constant flashes and there was the distant sound of many aircraft engines and explosions.
>
> 'It must be Coventry they're bombing,' my father said. And that went on for most of the night.

Audrey's father was right, as they found out the next day. By pure chance, that was the day they took a bus to Worcester, to get away from the bombing of Birmingham. And one of its regular stops on the way was Coventry:

> The driver drove very slowly through the horror of its bombed-out streets. Everywhere there was broken glass, rubble, ruined buildings, ARP and ambulance men desperately searching, fires still burning and people just wandering about – dazed.
>
> 'Oh, my God. Even the cathedral's gone!' Daddy said, sadly. Like everyone else on the bus, he was terribly upset.
>
> Then some people got off the bus, presumably because they lived there. And then, and I'll always remember this, passengers put their hands out to them sympathetically as they passed. 'Dear God, what are they going to find?' asked Mummy, tearfully. 'They might have lost everything!'
>
> And many of them probably had.

And that was how the Blitz had devastating effects on three English cities, Bristol, London and Coventry. There was horrific physical destruction, during which houses, streets and whole communities were more or less razed to the ground. There was also injury and death, and deep psychological trauma to the people who lived through the experience. And the people who were most deeply affected were, in many cases, women.

5

Death and Destruction

HOW BEING BOMBED BECAME A WAY OF LIFE

The bombing of Britain's ports and big industrial cities started in the summer of 1940 and continued until well into 1943. A fortunate few were able to get away from the bombing but for most people, sheltering became almost a way of life. And many women had tales to tell about what it was like.

The Fear Factor

Many women described how, perhaps surprisingly, they did not experience fear while they were being bombed. **Lorna Green** was a student in Bristol when she wrote, in a letter to her mother:

The first day raid warning was when I was out with my school-friend Averine. We were starting to eat large creamy pastry cakes when we heard many whistles by which we understood that there was about to be an air raid. We were just petrified by the

Lorna Green when she was a medical student at the University of Bristol.

thought that we were about to be done out of our tea! Eventually we went down to a shelter. Then we sat there and after half an hour we began to play a game, but before the all-clear had gone we went up and finished our tea. I never even heard a siren and no bombs were dropped. Very dull.

Later, in another letter, **Lorna** wrote:

The first night-raid in Bristol was a mild affair and I stayed awake reading Jane Austen until it was over. She had managed to ignore the Napoleonic War in her novels and I too could retreat for a while.

Ruby Spragg was also relatively fearless, even when the bombs really started falling. She worked at the Wills Tobacco Factory during the early bombing of Bristol:

The air raids were, in some ways, almost a welcome break. When the siren sounded we always used to switch off our machines and make our way down to the shelter in the basement. It was all very orderly — there was no rush, no panic. After a time, we just got used to it, although some of the girls I worked with were really scared. But I don't think I was, or at least I didn't want anyone to know I was. And that Wills Factory where I worked was such a huge building I felt much safer there than at home when the bombs were falling. I suppose it was a case of safety in numbers.

Patricia Roffe left school at 14 and started work in a factory, although the factory (Peek Frean's in Bermondsey) made biscuits, not cigarettes:

When the bombs started falling, we sheltered in a big storeroom surrounded by huge stacks of boxes, and sometimes they really started to sway. If they'd actually fallen I might have been buried alive under a mountain of Day-by-Day Assorted biscuits! But I don't think I was really scared. It was all quite exciting really. We just left it to the adults to be scared for us.

Elizabeth Longney had also left school and started work as a telephonist:

Working where I did, I was right in the middle of the Blitz on Bristol. When the sirens went we just had to put on a tin hat and make sure our gas

The bomb damage to the area near where **Elizabeth Longney** worked in the central telephone exchange. (© David Facey. Facey Collection. Bristol Archives: 41969/1/9)

masks were to hand and carry on working until a supervisor told us to go down to the deep shelter in the basement. But strangely enough, I don't think I was ever really scared – I was always one of the last to go down into the shelter. At that age you think you're immortal I suppose, and I just told myself that the noise of the explosions was a very bad thunderstorm and it would soon pass.

Dorothy Jones was less sanguine but still not really fearful, 'We used to talk quite a lot while the bombs were falling. We'd say things like, "My God, that was a big one!", "I wonder where that one landed?" and "How much longer is this going on?"'

Greta Cockaday also remembered that she wasn't really scared during the Blitz on London:

When there was a bombing raid, I think we all just took it in our stride. When the sirens went we didn't hurry to the shelters. There was no sense of panic, we just seemed to amble, as though we were on a picnic!

During night raids I remember there was a big brick shelter in our road which had bunks in it. I used to sleep in the top bunk with a neighbour below me. He snored very loudly so I had a bit of fun and I leaned over the side of my bunk and pulled his hair. That shut him up!

Other women had similarly light-hearted memories, although some bordered on the incredible. **Barbara Steadman** said:

One funny thing I remember at that time was a particularly bad bombing raid where the blast from the exploding bombs was enough to blow the feathers off the chickens in a smallholding, just near to where we lived. Some local people took pity on the featherless chickens and knitted little jackets for them! That was the story I heard anyway.

Dorothy Kears said:

For me, war wasn't something to be taken seriously. It was just a big adventure. Even when Bristol was being badly bombed I don't think I was scared. 'Isn't this fun?' we used to say to each other, and I remember laughing as the bombs were falling all around us.

How Anderson Shelters Became Unpopular
As time moved on, the unpopularity of Anderson shelters became almost universal. **Barbara Steadman** had this to say:

I hated going down into that shelter. It was cold and damp and dark and, worst of all, it was full of spiders. I've always hated spiders ever since! Eventually, we decided to take shelter in the big, tall cupboards in our ground-floor flat. We had pillows and blankets in there and it was far more comfortable and warmer than the shelter outside.

Dorothy Jones was living in the Wirral at this time, overlooking the heavily bombed Liverpool Docks:

The corrugated iron roof of our shelter used to leak and there used to be ankle-deep muddy puddles on the floor. It was also terribly crowded when our neighbours joined us – they didn't have a shelter of their own. We all had to sit facing each other with our elbows and knees touching.

I hated it down there. It was cold, damp, dirty and smelly, and when the sirens went it was terribly tempting to just stay in my lovely warm bed and hope for the best. But I didn't – well, not always.

Myrtle Young was less negative:

I was only 7 and I remember my mum made our Anderson shelter quite homely with cushions on the two benches and a curtain over the door. During the day, we used to use it as our playhouse.

Dorothy Jones, who developed a strong dislike of Anderson shelters.

But **Myrtle** was the exception. As a result of this almost universal unpopularity, shelter discipline became more and more lax. Thousands of people chose to stay in bed and hope for the best; a survey in the spring of 1941 concluded that during air raids only 51 per cent of families in Britain's cities took shelter. The majority of the population had developed a stubborn, fatalistic attitude to sheltering which could either be described as foolhardy or brave and defiant.

BOMBING RAIDS REMEMBERED

Particular raids were described by many women. On Friday, 11 April 1941 came one of the most devastating raids of all on Bristol. **HJF** wrote:

Good Friday. Sirens went at 9.45 tonight and now we are having a most terrible air raid.

Daddy was busy all night putting out incendiary bomb dropped in our garden and in our neighbours'.

Mr Churchill is said to be in Bristol, viewing the damage.

Eleanor Frost also described this raid:

> The most terrifying experience of all. Jerry came over and bombed us again
> here in the city centre. After enduring that horror for two hours the All
> Clear went, but fifteen minutes afterwards the Alert sounded again, and we
> had it even worse.
>
> At about midnight we each had a brandy and soda, and not a weak one! I
> find that I still shake though I no longer feel sick I am glad to say. Edith says
> she shakes too though without feeling very nervous. I do not feel as nervous
> as in the beginning of them in 1940 so I suppose we are all tougher though
> what a relief it will be when the All-clear goes at the end of the war!

But this wasn't the last raid **Eleanor Frost** experienced. On 26 April 1942
she wrote:

> I had just got into bed at 10.45 when the sirens went. Almost immedi-
> ately the guns started so out I got and bundled a few belongings and went
> downstairs to see how Mother was. She was awake and so I got into bed
> with her. Soon Mr Oscroft and then Edith came down dressed to go out
> and with their tin helmets on. The gun fire was a continuous roar which
> shook the house. I found it comforting and reassuring in a way as one does
> not hear other sounds so easily. The raid was on Bath [12 miles to the east
> of Bristol]. Edith has tried to get through to Mr Oxley but there is a delay
> of 3 hours … Mr Oxley rang up. He sounded old and a bit broken. He said
> Bath was a pitiable sight. There was a second air raid on the Sunday night.
> The Germans tried to destroy the city by fire. They also dive-bombed the
> people as they rushed to shelters and the firemen at their work.
>
> On Monday and Tuesday they were still digging out the victims of
> Saturday night's raid. One foreman saw a cat go into a hole in a demolished
> house and put in his hand to drag it back. To his horrified astonishment he
> felt his hand seized by a child's. We hear that 500 houses were destroyed and
> 10,000 damaged. Even the lovely and historic Assembly Rooms have been
> burnt out. It is a terrible act of destruction on a gem-like and perfect city with
> no military objectives. It was full of evacuees and refugees from other cities.

Up to this point, Bath had been relatively unscathed. But then it experienced what became known as a 'Baedeker raid' – the name given by the

German Propaganda Ministry to raids on historic cities with no particular military significance. In a memorable announcement, the ministry declared, 'We shall go out and bomb every building in cities marked with three stars in the *Baedeker Guide*'. The cities were Bath, Exeter, Norwich, York and Canterbury.

These German raids were said to be in retaliation for highly destructive raids by the RAF on the historic mediaeval German cities of Lübeck and Rostock. They followed the British Government's Area Bombing Directive, which first authorised the targeting of civilian areas.

As an afterword to this entry, **HJF** wrote on 30 April:

An unknown little girl died at the Bristol Royal Infirmary as a result of the air raid on Bath and no relation has come forward so she is to be buried in a nameless grave. Poor little mite!

Other women remembered particular air raids. **Audrey Swindells** was 11 and living with her family in the Camp Hill area of Birmingham, near the main railway station, an area often targeted by German bombers:

One morning, just after my father had cycled off to work at the nearby Lucas Small-Arms Factory, my mother was clearing away our breakfast when she looked out of the window and suddenly cried out, 'Oh no!'

I rushed to look and there were a lot of policemen and soldiers about and the road outside was cordoned off. 'Get your hat and coat. We're not staying here,' she said, as she was putting hers on. When we got downstairs and opened the front door, a policeman stood there saying, 'And where do you think you're going?'

'To my sister's,' my mother answered.

'There are two unexploded bombs out here and we're waiting for the bomb disposal team,' said the policeman.

'Well!' said my mother in a very determined way, 'We're not waiting here for those to go off!' My mother really was a very determined woman when she wanted to be.

'Well,' said the policeman, 'If you're prepared to risk it and run quickly, you can go now.'

So we ran, seeing the two big bombs in the holes as we passed. It was very scary and very dramatic.

LUCKY ESCAPES

Close-ups with the Enemy

It would be completely wrong to think that during the Second World War it was just the men in the armed services who risked their lives, came close to being seriously injured or even killed. Several of the women I spoke to experienced lucky escapes, some of them extremely lucky. Many were as a result of being bombed, others for different reasons.

In the summer of 1940, **Diana England** was still living at home with her parents and several servants in their large country house in Berkshire:

> One night my mother rushed into my bedroom shouting, 'Get up quickly. A plane has crashed into our garden!' My mother then pushed me and the maids into the cellar before she went to answer a knock at the door. It was our young female air-raid warden, who very excitedly said, 'A German bomber has crashed into your garden and the crew have parachuted down and we don't know where they are.'
>
> So there we were, in real danger from the German crew of the crashed bomber. Of course we checked that all the doors and windows were locked before eventually we all went back to bed – although not to sleep. Then, early next morning, Bernice, one of our maids, took my brother Tony's shotgun and went all round the garden. I thought that was awfully brave of her.
>
> In fact, the German crew had given themselves up very quickly to the local Home Guard, all, that is, except for one member of the crew, Josef Markl, who hid and didn't give himself up until eight days later.

Cynthia Ellis lived in the small village of Aveton Gifford in south Devon:

> You wouldn't think it would be a dangerous place to live, would you? But on 26 January 1943, our village was attacked. I was 9 years old at the time and I remember coming home from school and then walking with my friend Pauline Moor and our two dolls' prams to the village shop on Fore Street. That was about 50 yards away from where I lived – and still do.
>
> Anyway, I remember we were both looking in the shop window when we heard a tremendous roaring noise coming up the valley. It got louder and louder until I saw that it was a plane, flying very fast and very low, and on the side of that plane was a big black cross. In fact, it was so low and so near to where we were standing we could see the pilot's head with his leather helmet on.

Then we saw a big bomb dropping from underneath the plane, which immediately climbed as fast as it could to get away from the blast of the bomb exploding. In fact the bomb hit the rectory, which was just on the other side of the brook less than 100 yards away from where we were standing. It was a direct hit and the whole house went up and it was almost completely destroyed.

Cynthia Ellis.

When we saw this happening, we just ran as fast as we could into the village shop. But Mrs Steer, the lady who owned the shop, wasn't there, she was in her back garden. So we took shelter in her kitchen until she came in from the garden and pushed us behind a big arm-chair in the corner. 'We must say the Lord's Prayer,' she said. So we did. And then when we'd finished saying the Lord's Prayer we said to her, 'What shall we do now then, Mrs Steer?'

'Say it again,' she said. And then after that there was silence, I remember.

Later, when we came out of the shop, the first person we saw was Myrtle Moor, Pauline's mother. She was covered in blood. And then my mother came running up Fore Street looking for me and she was covered in blood too. She was terribly upset because she didn't know where I was and even if I was still alive. But for some reason, I didn't cry and I didn't even feel frightened. It's strange, that …

Next, I remember that Fore Street was in a terrible state. There was mud everywhere, broken glass, bricks and slates from the roofs of lots of houses. And oddest of all was the sight of eels and old bicycles from the brook hanging over the telephone wires.

Back at home, our house was also in a terrible state. Another German plane had flown down Fore Street while we were hiding behind Mrs Steer's armchair, machine gunning everything on its way, and that included our house. All our windows were broken and bullets had come through one window which faced up the street and had ended up lodged in our piano on the other side of the room. One bullet stayed there for years!

Meanwhile, in the rectory things were really bad. A little girl was killed there and she was my cousin. Her name was Sonia Weeks and people said that her mother suffocated her daughter because she was holding her too tight, trying to protect her from the exploding bomb. Another terrible thing happened that afternoon – our village church was badly damaged by another German bomb. I'll never forget that afternoon. Never!

The parish church of Aveton Gifford after the raid on 26 January 1943. (Courtesy of St Andrew's Church, Aveton Gifford)

The church as it is now.

Like **Cynthia, Audrey Swindells** also saw a German pilot close up. She was just returning home after being told to leave because of two unexploded bombs in her road (see page 97):

> Seeing that the police cordons had gone, my mother was just saying, 'It must be safe now' when we heard a very low-flying aircraft. We looked up and it was flying right above us and, to my horror, I saw swastikas on the wings and we could also see the pilot in his leather headgear and goggles. The next minute, we were pushed down from behind and then a man, a warden, held us and said, 'He's gone, but if he comes back don't look up. Just lie flat on your faces! Don't you realise he might have strafed you?' As we both looked puzzled, he added in an irritated way. 'Machine-gunned!' he said.

Sheila Kellard had a remarkably similar experience to this:

> I was walking along our road on the way home from school in Bristol when I heard the sound of an aircraft flying very low. Of course, I thought it was one of ours but then I saw that it had a black cross on the side and as it came towards me it started firing at me, so I instinctively ran as fast as I could in a zigzag to try and avoid the bullets hitting me. Then I flung myself in the gutter just as two bullets buried themselves in a tree just above my head.

Lucky to Survive

Some women also described events that they, or members of their family, were lucky to survive. **Pam Allcock** was the daughter of a vet who lived and worked in the centre of Bristol during the worst of the bombing. She recounted how her father was particularly lucky to survive:

> One night during the Bristol Blitz, my father's surgery in 13 Berkeley Square received a direct hit. The same bomb also destroyed the YWCA house next door with catastrophic consequences – thirty-four girls were killed. At the time, my father's secretary, Mrs Jones, his kennelman Frank and my father were all sheltering down in the basement which they thought was the safest place to be.
>
> My father, who'd come down last, was on one side of the room and the other two were sitting opposite. By a massive stroke of good fortune, the

door which my father had just shut behind him was blown open and fell across his body and protected him from the full weight of the rubble that fell all around him. The other two were both killed outright. Incredibly, my father survived, although he was buried under the rubble for over fifteen hours. Rescue workers arriving at the scene of total destruction assumed that everyone in the building must have been killed so went off to search through the remains of buildings less seriously damaged.

The next morning another rescue worker was climbing over the huge pile of rubble that was all that remained of No. 13 when he just heard a faint tapping sound. Other rescue workers joined him and after digging for hours, they finally found my father. He'd been pinned down but he could just move one arm enough to grab a kettle and use that to make the tapping noise which eventually guided rescuers to where he was buried. We learned later that it took the rescuers five bowls of water to wash his face because the dirt was so deeply ingrained. He was quite badly injured – he had nearly lost the use of his legs – so of course they took him straight to hospital.

My poor mother knew nothing of what had happened to him but persuaded our fire warden to drive her round from hospital to hospital trying desperately to find him. She must have been frantic with worry. When she eventually found him, he was still covered in filth and mud, shouting, 'Phone my wife! Tell her to get the children out of Bristol!' And that's what happened. [See page 61 for **Pam**'s experiences as an evacuee.]

Pam went on to describe another earlier time when she was perhaps lucky to survive. She was living with her parents in the large house in Berkeley Square which was destroyed soon after that. On the top floor of the house they had a lodger, a musician by the name of Bernard Tigh:

One night, an incendiary device came crashing through our roof and landed on the bedroom floor of Bernard Tigh. My mother and I happened to be in the room at the time looking out of the bedroom window at the raid in progress, although he himself was out fire watching. Anyway, we were trapped in the room with the smoking incendiary device between us and the bedroom door. The only thing we could do was grab piles of sheet music which Bernard Tigh had stacked on his chest of drawers. We hoped that the sheer weight of all that paper would put the fire out. Fortunately, it did and we were just able to jump over the pile of smouldering papers and get to the door.

A warden searching for survivors in the ruins of a house, similar to the search for **Pam Allcock's** father, who was very nearly buried alive. (© David Facey. Facey Collection. Bristol Archives: 41969/1/4)

Unfortunately, there was a rumour afterwards that my mother was so panic-stricken that she desperately threw paper on the fire to try and put it out. That wasn't the whole truth, of course.

Rosemary Strydom came from the Pimlico area, near Victoria station in London, where her mother had a B&B business. The family also had another property:

It was a small wooden bungalow on an island in the middle of the Thames near Shepperton and we sometimes used to cycle there for the weekend. On the morning of Monday, 16 October 1940, we returned to our house in Pimlico only to find the police had barricaded off our street. An enormous parachute mine had exploded nearby and destroyed or badly damaged 150 houses. Twenty-three people were killed and sixty badly injured and over 300 people were made homeless, including ourselves. All our furniture and possessions, photographs and clothes were completely destroyed, including my birth certificate, which was to be significant later [see page 125]. So we just had to get on our bikes and cycle back to our bungalow in Shepperton.

Lorna McNab described one particular occasion when she and her family were also very lucky to survive. They lived on one floor of a five-storey house in Clifton, Bristol, and they used to shelter in the cellar:

We heard the whistle of a bomb falling. By then, my mother was in the front cellar room putting on a pair of slacks, as we used to call them in those days. She had one leg in and one leg out when the bomb exploded, actually in the courtyard of our house, on the other side of the wall. The blast blew her right across the room. How she wasn't seriously hurt, I'll never know.

My father, meanwhile, had just come down the stairs to the cellar at the moment the bomb exploded and the whole lot came crashing down behind him, staircase and all. The enormous black curtain which hung at the foot of the stairs fell and enveloped him – it was that that saved him from being seriously injured. We then all crawled over piles of rubble out onto the street.

The next day, we saw the devastation to the house we lived in. The windows were all missing and the balcony had collapsed. The floorboards had all been lifted by the blast and my parents' best china was completely smashed. We couldn't carry on living there – it was uninhabitable. But we couldn't leave immediately because our cat and dog, Flip and Ted, were looking down at us from where the windows of our flat had been and there was no way of reaching them because the staircase had collapsed. The emergency services were far too busy to come and rescue a couple of pets so my mother called the Boy Scouts and they climbed a ladder and rescued them.

But, unfortunately, the blast from the bomb caused my pet goldfish to be blown right out of his bowl and I never did find out where he landed.

Irene Stunt was living in a flat in East Dulwich, a relatively safe suburb of south London, well away from the worst of the Blitz – except that, between January and May 1944, the Luftwaffe mounted a second bombing campaign, which Londoners called the 'Baby Blitz'. With her husband David away fighting in North Africa and then Italy, she was sharing the flat with a female friend, Pat James. Irene had a daughter, Angela, who was seventeen months old at the time. Living just up the same road were Irene's parents.

David and **Irene Stunt** on their wedding day in June 1941.

Irene takes up the story:

I remember we heard the air-raid siren go, which was unusual at that stage of the war – 28 March 1944 it was. Anyway, we had a Morrison shelter in the kitchen/dining room of our flat which was a sort of metal cage.

Then, suddenly, BOOM! A bomb fell right on top of the house we were living in. It was a direct hit. There was broken glass and debris everywhere and Pat was badly hurt. She had blood all over her face and she'd lost a finger. But by some miracle, I wasn't injured at all and neither apparently was my baby daughter, Angela. I picked her up but then I realised that, to my horror, she was quite lifeless. I ran out of the house and up the road to my parents' with Angela in my arms, screaming, 'She's dead! She's dead!' all the way.

Later, the coroner decided that it was the blast from the bomb that had killed her.

Irene ended her story, 'I didn't go to her funeral. I just couldn't. I've always said that if I had gone I would have thrown myself into the grave with her.'

Irene Stunt and her daughter, Angela, who was killed in a bombing raid on south London on 28 March 1944.

Rosemary Strydom was serving in the ATS (Auxiliary Territorial Service) in London when she described an event she was lucky to survive. She was living in a large house in Belgravia, near to where she was working as a clerk with the Grenadier Guards:

> At 11.20 a.m. on Sunday, 18 June 1944, one of the very first V1s, or doo-dlebug bombs, fell directly onto the Guards Chapel, which was full of ATS girls, Grenadier Guards and civilians. 121 people in the chapel were killed and 141 seriously injured.
>
> It was extremely lucky that I wasn't in chapel that morning but it was only because we'd been told that attendance wasn't compulsory after a particularly heavy raid the night before and I'd decided to stay in bed.
>
> I knew several of the girls that were killed that morning. Some were good friends of mine.

Peggy Turner also described how V1s were extremely dangerous:

> I was living in Eltham, Kent, at the time, in what became known as 'Flying Bomb Alley'. I'll always remember hearing the drone of their engines and then suddenly the noise stopped which meant that the engine had cut out.

We then had the terrifying experience of waiting and waiting to find out where the bomb would fall.

In some ways, the V2s weren't so bad. You didn't hear them coming. You just heard a loud bang when they exploded. If you heard the bang, you were still alive!

Like **Rosemary** and **Peggy**, **Judith West** was also very fortunate to escape from a flying bomb. As a 7-year-old, she was living with her family in Welling, in Kent, which was in a direct line between the V1 launch sites and central London:

Towards the end of the war I'd just been bathed, I remember, and my mother was drying me in front of the fire when the French windows and the conservatory were all blown in by the blast from a flying bomb which had exploded only two streets away. I was rushed to a First Aid station, where I was given a cup of tea with lots of condensed milk in it. Next morning, I went home and there was still blood everywhere – my blood – all over my parents' precious three-piece suite!

Suzanne Best was also lucky to survive the explosion of a V1. She was 16 and at a girls' school just outside Portsmouth:

I remember I was sitting a French School Certificate exam in the examination hall and I was writing away in French as best I could when I heard the unmistakable sound of a German doodlebug getting closer and closer. The sound got louder and louder and then suddenly stopped. That silence was the most terrifying experience I had during the entire war. I just had time for a very slow intake of breath, then I held it for a moment, waiting to find out where it was going to fall or whether I was going to live or die! Then I remember we all put our pens down and dived for cover under our desks!

In fact, it exploded close by with a very big bang and left a huge hole in the ground. I almost wanted to laugh with the feeling of relief but I couldn't – I had a French exam to finish! We were then told to pick up our pens and carry on as if nothing had happened.

The dangers did not discriminate between women or men, young or old. The high-explosive bombs that fell out of the sky and incredibly destructive fires, started by incendiaries and later V1 and V2 rockets, were all responsible for killing or horribly injuring huge numbers of people, irrespective of their gender or age. Their stories are just a few examples that show just how lucky thousands were to escape with their lives.

To sum up, the Blitz affected most of the big industrial cities but the scale of London's devastation outweighed any other. Between September 1940 and May 1941, London saw 19,877 civilian deaths and 25,578 serious casualties – just over half the total for the whole country. And around a quarter of a million houses were destroyed or badly damaged.

But to put these grim statistics into a different context, the German air raids on Britain were not indiscriminate but targeted, for the most part, on ports, factories, warehouses and railway infrastructure. In contrast, RAF raids on Germany were far less accurate and specific in their targets. Arthur 'Bomber' Harris, commander-in-chief of Bomber Command, ordered the systematic destruction of whole German towns and cities by RAF night-time bombing raids in which as many as 1,000 aircraft took part. It was a strategy called 'area bombing', designed to 'de-house' as many people as possible and so destroy German morale. Harris announced:

> We are going to scourge the Third Reich from end to end. We are bombing Germany, city by city, and ever more terribly in order to make it impossible for her to go on with the war. That is our object and we shall pursue it relentlessly.

The US Air Force went along with this strategy, which resulted in approximately 410,000 civilians being killed by the Allied bombing of Germany. Many historians argue that it was a strategy that largely failed.

Similarly, the Luftwaffe's bombing campaign, which started out as the military tactic that would rapidly bring Britain to its knees, also proved to be a failure – just. Against expectations, civilian morale cracked but did not collapse and Britain was not demoralised into surrender. And war production, despite extensive damage to factories, actually went up, partly due to the planned dispersal of production to shadow factories all over the country and also the huge-scale recruitment of women to work in those factories.

As far as Bristol is concerned, there is still, even today, plenty of evidence of the mass destruction that was caused. The author's own house is just next to a children's playground built on the site of two houses that were destroyed by a bombing raid. And in the graveyard behind St Mary Redcliffe Church, there is a tramline sticking out from the ground at an angle of 45 degrees, blown sky-high during a bombing raid. It was left where it landed as a kind of memorial. The inscription beside it reads:

On Good Friday 11th April 1941 this tramline was thrown over the adjoining houses by a high explosive bomb which fell on Redcliffe Hill. It is left to remind us how narrowly the church escaped destruction in the war 1939–1945.

The tramline in the churchyard of St Mary Redcliffe Church, Bristol.

The so-called 'Blitz spirit' has often been invoked, but the reality was not a tale of unalloyed resilience and heroism. There was a lot of looting after bombing raids left houses wide open. And many thousands of householders became 'trekkers' as they joined convoys leaving the big cities, trusting their neighbours to remove the incendiaries which threatened to burn their houses down.

Eleanor Frost summed up how she felt after a particular raid finally ended:

> The sense of relief! And soon after that I heard the first cheep of birds and the dawn chorus coincided with the 'All Clear'. What a curious juxtaposition of sounds. The world as it might be and the world as it is!

To end this chapter on a more positive note, there was an overwhelming community spirit during the Blitz. People, in the main, were generous, supportive and caring towards each other and this often extended to total strangers. **Rose Jennings** described what it was like when the All-Clear sounded, 'The Blitz had an extraordinary effect on the people who lived through it. Everyone used to come out and talk to complete strangers. There was a great feeling of camaraderie and solidarity – it was lovely.'

Ruby Spragg also summed up similar feelings about being blitzed, 'The thing about being in the war, especially when we were being bombed, was a great feeling of togetherness. We cared for each other and took care of each other. It was a good feeling, a good spirit.'

6

Called Up!

During the First World War, girls and women were, for the most part, only expected to keep the home fires burning. There were of course exceptions – thousands worked as nurses or filled shells in munitions factories, although none were conscripted. But in the Second World War, things were very different. A huge number of girls and young women volunteered or were conscripted into one of the armed services and many more were effectively conscripted to do war work.

Of the three services, the WRNS (Women's Royal Naval Service) was generally thought of as the most prestigious. They were certainly the most selective – only 80,000 WRNS, popularly known as Wrens, were enrolled during the war, compared to 185,000 WAAFs (Women's Auxiliary Air Force) and the 222,000 who served in the ATS – they seemingly had a more relaxed selection policy.

For most women, conscription was not an unwelcome example of state interference and compulsion. It was more often a welcome opportunity to get away from tight parental control and, in many cases, poor housing conditions. Just the idea of having your own bed, wearing clean clothes, having three square meals a day and getting paid – albeit not much – was immensely attractive to hundreds of thousands of young women. Added to which, life in the services meant freedom to meet, go out with and have fun with young men.

Ivy Rogers was typical of the women I interviewed who volunteered for one of the services. After working for two years in the Wills Cigarette Factory in Bristol, she decided to join the WRNS. With every sailor needed to man the navy's warships, the WRNS started advertising for recruits with pictures of smiling, attractive women in front of a fluttering Red Ensign and, for good measure, a destroyer at sea in the background.

That was the fantasy. The reality was usually very different. There were thousands of mundane jobs previously done by men – jobs like stores assistant, driver, telephonist, clerk and cook. Another advertisement was much more honest. Its headline was, 'Join the Wrens and Free a Man for the Fleet'.

Recruitment was sometimes problematic. Another slogan, 'Up with the lark and to bed with a Wren', perhaps illustrates the changing attitudes presented as a result of the realities of war. Young men and women, away from home for the first time, facing very real life-threatening situations, seized their opportunities to live life to the full.

Ivy Rogers, who spent most of the war as a cook in the WRNS.

Ivy had a good reason for choosing the WRNS:

My dad was a tugboat captain, so of course I wanted to do a job which had something to do with boats, and I asked to work on the mail boats, delivering mail to warships just coming into port. But unfortunately, they just said they might transfer me later. They never did!

So then I went up to London to do my basic training. I was fitted out with a uniform and I thought I looked very smart because I used to have my detachable white collars properly washed and starched at a Chinese laundry back home. I was very proud of my uniform!

The WRNS then decided that I'd make a good cook, so they trained me to work in what they called the galley, to make good plain food. My mum had already taught me how to cook so I didn't find it difficult.

The other girl volunteers were from all over the country – I was the only one from Bristol. I remember the girls from London were the loudest and the cheekiest. They were know-alls, they were. I was never mouthy like them. My best friend was from Yorkshire. She was young like me but she was already a widow. Her husband was a sailor and he'd been drowned.

I'll always remember one evening we went out together into the West End of London. We were both wearing a pair of Kayser Bondor stockings with a seam up the back, for the very first time. Anyway, we had a wonderful time – but I won't tell you what we got up to – and then we got completely lost in the blackout!

After that I was sent to the South Western Hotel, which was on the dockside in Southampton, next to the main railway station. It used to be a luxury hotel but it had been taken over by the navy in 1940 and renamed HMS *Shrapnel*. Some of the rooms were still very grand but behind the scenes, where I was working, it was filthy with cockroaches everywhere and rats. Anyway, I was good at my job so I was soon promoted to Officers' Cook.

While I was there, I could eat as much food as I liked despite strict food rationing. But because it was always there I didn't eat much. I started out in the Wrens weighing 10st 8lbs and ended up 8st 10lbs.

The South Western Hotel, Southampton, renamed HMS *Shrapnel* by the Royal Navy, where **Ivy Rogers** lived and worked as a cook.

At that time, I was friends with another Wren who worked as a sick-berth attendant. We used to swap. I gave her food and she used to give me brown bandages and I sent these home to my mum. I've still got some upstairs. I also used to fill cocoa tins full of dripping and send those home to my mum in the post. It's funny to remember what things were in short supply because of rationing …

I might have been living in what was a luxury hotel but, can you believe it, we were only allowed one bath a week and the water had to be no more than five inches deep. And to make sure we didn't break that rule, there was a black line all the way round the bath at a height of five inches and an officer could come in at any time.

While I was there in Southampton I had compassionate leave because my dad was very ill. I went back to Bristol and spent the weekend with him. I said goodbye at the end of my leave and got on the train. He died before I got back to Southampton. He was only 46. I still miss him.

The novelist **Pat Barker** also described how her mother was in the WRNS:

She was stationed in Dunfermline and she talked enthusiastically about the war. It was the best time of her life; it was dynamic, she joined the forces, she left home. She was with large numbers of women, many of them from different walks of society, so it was a kind of education for her. She believed absolutely in what we were fighting for, as the vast majority of people did, of course. She just had a thoroughly good time.

But then, amid the dancing with Polish officers, my mother became pregnant, giving birth to me in 1943. But I never knew who my father was and I honestly don't believe my mother had any real memory of who he was, or anything about him.[1]

Pat's mother's experience of joining one of the services and becoming pregnant was not particularly uncommon.

Diana England also volunteered, but for the WAAFs not the WRNS:

My friend Penelope said that she was going to volunteer and that sounded frightfully exciting. So we went into Reading together, which is where all the recruiting offices were. But I was never in any doubt that I wanted to

---

1   Interview in *The Guardian* by Alex Clark on 29 August 2015.

join the WAAFs because I'd always been interested in planes since I was a little girl. It's funny that, isn't it? And anyway, I liked air force blue much more than khaki or navy blue.

After that, the only big question was whether I should try to become an officer or stay an AC2, the lowest rank in the WAAFs. Anyway, despite the fact that I'd been head girl at my boarding school, I decided that if I became an officer they'd probably want me to train as a plotter, moving symbols for incoming German bombers with long sticks across a huge horizontal map. But I was terribly nervous that if I made a mistake it would have disastrous consequences. So I applied to be a clerk AC2 instead. My mother wasn't best pleased.

In March 1942, I was sent to a camp in Gloucestershire and as soon as we got there we had to have an FFI (Free From Infection) inspection, which involved stripping off down to our underwear and being checked for nits and so on. We used to call them 'Flying Flea Inspections'. I remember the girl next to me, who came from London, was obviously from a very poor background and was having terrible difficulty because her dress was so filthy it practically stuck to her. So she asked me to help her take it off. I did, of course, and after that she offered to share her bag of chips with me and we became very good friends. I remember I used to help her write letters home.

As a postscript to this story, **Diana** told me that while she was in hospital a month or so later:

My friend from London, the one who I'd helped at the FFI inspection, came to see me. She told me that she was pregnant and asked me if I would be willing to be the baby's godmother. Of course I said I'd love to. But when the WAAFs discovered she was pregnant she was discharged under Clause 11 and unfortunately I lost touch with her. So I never did become a godmother.

The FFI inspection was well remembered by many women. One described it thus:

There must have been 300 of us, jostled together and lost. A woman's voice bawled at us to take our clothes off and line up with our arms in the air. Then, when it was my turn, a medical orderly jerked my head forward, parted my hair, inspected my underarms and then my pubic hair. This ritual humiliation took less than a minute. Thankfully, I passed inspection and was ordered to get dressed. It was then that I noticed that half the girls had been isolated into a separate group. I asked a WAAF corporal why and was told that most of them had nits and a few crabs but that we were a clean lot compared to some.

Another woman described the same experience:

When we first got there, we were all in civilian clothes and we were sent to an enormous warehouse with a huge heap of uniforms piled up on the floor in the middle. A corporal then shouted at us, 'Right, grab a uniform and get changed. At the double!' Well, I found that really embarrassing, I think we all did. So we just turned our backs, faced the wall, hurriedly took everything off without looking at each other and put on the uniform which happened to be next on the pile. Needless to say, it didn't fit.

Diana England then went on to describe her training:

I was then kitted out with my uniform. I was very proud of it and I used to enjoy polishing my buttons. I thought I looked really smart. It certainly made a change from the Aertex shirts and jodhpurs I used to wear as a girl.

Then I was sent to Morecombe in Lancashire. We were billeted in seaside boarding houses, four to a room, which was not at all what I was used to! The other three girls were from all over the country and were from very ordinary backgrounds. But we all got on extremely well. I thought I might be picked on because I spoke with an 'Oxford accent', as it was called in those days, but

Diana England was very proud of her WAAF's uniform.

not a bit of it. They were, without exception, awfully friendly and kind to me.

The basic training consisted mainly of learning how to march and salute. We also had to get reasonably fit so we had PT sessions on the beach and went on long route marches. We were taught by a woman sergeant – I think we were all a bit frightened of her. But I enjoyed the drilling, getting the timing right.

Unfortunately, at the end of my basic training, we had vaccinations against smallpox and the next day I felt absolutely ghastly and I was delirious so they sent me to an isolation hospital. I had a bad bout of vaccine fever. I was in hospital for two or three weeks while all my new friends had left Morecombe and been posted to an aerodrome at Upper Heyford near Oxford, leaving me behind.

When I got better, I travelled to Upper Heyford by train, on my own, and when I arrived at the nearest station I naively expected some form of transport to be waiting to take me to the camp. But there was nothing and the porter told me I'd have to hitch-hike. I'd never hitch-hiked in my life before!

So I just stood by the side of the road until an open lorry came past and I waved it down. It was full of young RAF airmen from the base. The next thing I knew, they were pulling me up into the lorry and I was sitting in the middle of them, on their knees! My mother would have been horrified. Half an hour later, I was back in a big Nissen hut with all my friends from Morecombe. I was so happy!

That was my first experience of hitch-hiking, but it certainly wasn't my last. While I was in the WAAFs I had forty-eight hours' leave every three months and I always used to hitch-hike home on my own. Having a uniform seemed to help.

Upper Heyford was perfect. It was a real aerodrome with a control tower, lots of different planes, a long runway and hangars. They were training young pilots to fly there, first using small trainers and later on Wellington bombers. I used to watch them learning how to take off and land and listening to shouts of 'Get that f*** tail up!' and things like that.

I was there during the winter of 1942, which I remember was freezing cold, and in desperation I used to heat up an electric iron and wrap it in my woollen WAAF stockings and take it to bed with me as a kind of hot-water bottle. I also used to wear in bed a thick woollen cricket sweater – a present from my brother who went to Eton – and the other girls used to tease me with shouts of 'Who are you playing for tonight then Diana?'

One of my jobs at Upper Heyford was to keep the logbooks up to date on each of the Wellington bombers on the base. To do that, I had to cycle round to all the planes at dispersal and make sure they were all fitted with the latest modifications and their Merlin engines were not flying more than 300 hours. I got to know a lot of the fitters and pilots very well.

I remember my mother worried about me in the company of so many men of other ranks. In fact, she drove up to see me once and gave me a Boy Scout's knife to use if I should ever be attacked while I was out on my bicycle. 'Go for their private parts!' she advised me!

After about two years at Upper Heyford, I was posted to the Records Office in Gloucester and was billeted with a WAAF friend, Isa, in a terraced house in the city. My accommodation there came as a bit of a shock. The house consisted of a parlour only used for 'company' and later for the baby's pram, then a kitchen and an outside WC. There were only two bedrooms upstairs and my friend and I shared one. There was no bathroom, so once a week our landlady – her name was Nancy – would light the copper and boil just enough water to fill a tin bath with hot, soapy water and then we'd take it in turns to have a bath.

Another thing, when my landlady's baby was on the way I could hear her screaming and I remember thinking that if that's how much it hurts, I never, ever want to have a baby myself. Anyway, I had to get on my bicycle to fetch the midwife. Of course, I changed my mind about having babies later!

I kept in touch with Nancy and they came to our family house in Berkshire when her son Keith was 20 – the baby I'd 'helped' to deliver.

Sadly, while I was in Gloucestershire my mother came to tell me that my brother Tony had been posted 'missing, believed killed' in North Africa. I'll always remember that when war was declared Tony said to me, 'Oh no, that's terrible news. I don't want to go and get killed!'

Anyway, his colonel wrote that he'd been shot while on patrol and was seen to fall but they never found his body. Although my mother made endless enquiries, we never heard any more so she never really believed he was dead and that he'd never come back. That was why we never moved house. She was very worried lest he return and discover different people living in his home and not be able to find us. [An internet search confirmed that Anthony Clive Uzielli, **Diana**'s brother, a lieutenant in the King's Royal Rifle Corps, was killed at Medjez-el-bab, Tunisia, on 26 April 1943.]

After the Records Office in Gloucester, I was moved again. My elder brother David, who was working in the code breaking establishment at Bletchley Park, managed to get me posted there. He was frightfully clever, unlike me, and he went to the University of Cambridge and was a real egghead, which was why he was code breaking at Bletchley Park.

Nobody was allowed to say a word about the work we were doing – I didn't even talk about it with my own brother, which was terribly difficult. I found out much later that David was working in a section that listened to messages from a different Enigma machine which was used by Hitler to communicate with his generals. But David never said a word about this. Similarly, when my mother travelled up to see me, I couldn't tell her anything about the work I was doing and when a boyfriend at the time came to see me and asked, 'Are you code breaking in there or something?', I had to pretend that I didn't know what he was talking about. I took it all very seriously.

I was obviously good at my job and after a while I was promoted to corporal and then to sergeant. The sergeants' mess was really wonderful, so much better than the other ranks' – much better food and a bar!

My job was simple once I'd learnt the Q code in which the German wireless operators communicated with each other. For example, 'I have a message for X Station', followed by a string of letters. Our own wireless operators would listen in to the enemy and copy down these coded messages and the results would arrive on my desk in the shape of 'logs' about 12in by 12in. Then I would copy out the messages and any relevant Q code.

I was told to try to find out if any message had been recorded and sent elsewhere. Now and then, a code breaker would come and read what I had recorded. I worked eight-hour shifts, which meant that I was sometimes eating my breakfast at midnight.

Before the war my parents had planned for me to go straight from boarding school to a very smart finishing school in Paris. But the war put paid to those plans and I ended up in the WAAFs instead, and I can honestly say that I learnt far, far more there, about myself and about real life, than I ever would have in a French finishing school for young ladies.

Greta Cockaday also joined the WAAFs. She was living and working in London and had two clerical jobs, both of them apparently boring, so according to **Greta**:

I went along to the WAAFs Recruiting Office and luckily enough I got the job I was hoping for – as a driver. I was sent up to Bridgenorth in Shropshire to do my basic training.

Not long after that I was issued with my uniform. I didn't mind the tie and the air-force-blue shirt and blouse and the peaked cap. But I did mind the passion killers, which we had to wear under our skirts. They came down to just above our knees. ['Passion killers' were standard-issue WAAF knickers.]

After basic training I did a Motor Transport Training Course in Morecombe. At first, I drove RAF cars, usually Hillmans and Standards. From cars, I graduated to driving lorries up to 30 cwt, although I could only just reach the pedals.

On one training exercise we had to drive in a convoy at night into the Lake District as far as Keswick, with only our side lights on, making sure that we kept the same distance behind the lorry in front. That wasn't easy because driving lorries was hard work compared to driving cars – the cab was draughty, noisy and uncomfortable and there was no synchromesh on the gears so we had to double de-clutch every time we changed gear. I passed that test and was promoted to ACW1.

After that I got my first real driving job. I was sent to an RAF airfield – Kemble, in Gloucestershire. My job was mainly to drive crews and supplies out to the aircraft dispersed all around the airfield. Sometimes I drove big, heavy lorries, sometimes ambulances, sometimes just cars.

Another of my jobs was to drive a flat-bed lorry to an ordnance depot 50 miles away. There they loaded it up with bombs and ammunition which I then had to drive back to Kemble. Looking back on it now, I suppose that was quite dangerous.

Every day was different, that's why I loved the job. And I got paid for doing it – not much but just enough for me to buy things like make-up and toothpaste. Everything else came with the job.

One of my regular driving jobs was to take the catering officer into the nearby town of Tetbury. I often used to end up with a big, juicy steak when I did that run – things like that just seemed to fall off the back of a lorry somehow.

On another occasion, I was told to pick up the commanding officer. He took one look at me and said, 'Where's my driver?'

'He's been posted away Sir. I'm your new driver.'

'I don't approve of women drivers!' he barked, but nevertheless got in.

He then proceeded to light a cigarette. A few moments later he said, 'Well, what are we waiting for?'

'I'm not going to leave until you put out your cigarette, Sir. With all this fuel and bombs and ammunition around, smoking is against regulations.'

There was a moment's silence before he put his cigarette out and I drove off. Funnily enough, he always asked for me to drive him after that.

In fact, I spent the rest of the war driving – I never bumped, let alone crashed a car or a lorry the whole time I was in the WAAFs. I enjoyed driving far more than sitting behind a desk. And I enjoyed the whole atmosphere in the WAAFs during the war. We were all on the same side, so close, such very good friends.

Joan Fell was another young woman who decided to join the WAAFs:

I joined because I wanted a bit of excitement and also because I loved my country and I wanted to do my bit. I was just 19 at the time. I didn't tell my mother because I knew she wouldn't approve. Sure enough, when she found out she was very cross and said to me, 'Be it on your head, girl!'

I was sent to Plymouth and there I had to choose between four different trades – cook, clerk, driver and batwoman – although we didn't really have much choice. We just stood in a line and they pointed at us in turn – there was nothing like an aptitude test or anything like that. Anyway, I was told I was going to be a clerk and I was happy enough with that.

The next thing was that I was given a train ticket and told to go to Weymouth. From there, I was taken in the back of a 4-ton lorry to my first posting – a fighter aerodrome called Warmwell, a few miles behind Weymouth and not far from the important naval base at Portland.

In fact, we were the first WAAFs on the station and there we were given our first RAF meal. It was a huge tin bath full of a stew of some description, which looked and smelled so disgusting that none of us wanted to even try it. We all preferred to go hungry rather than eat that stew. The little man who was ladling it out just shrugged his shoulders and said, 'All right girls. You'll soon get used to it.'

While I was at Warmwell, I became good friends with a lot of the pilots and one offered me a flight. I was smuggled out to his aircraft, a Fairey Battle it was, a light bomber with a three-man crew. I was told to keep my head down and stay out of sight. I didn't see very much.

Soon after that, Spitfires and Hurricanes arrived and took part in the Battle of Britain. The pilots were so young and so brave. I knew three of them in particular. They'd all trained together. But they were all shot down and killed within a few days of each other.

I was then posted to another aerodrome at Dumfries in Scotland. It was a training base, relatively safe from surprise attacks by German aircraft. I had a good time while I was there. I went to lots of parties, I remember. Once I was put on a charge because I came back late and every airman on the base came to look at me as I sat on a bench waiting to go into the group captain's office to be disciplined. Fortunately, I was let off with just a warning. And even after that, I frequently came back late to camp, lying on the back seat of a car, hidden under rugs.

While I was at Dumfries, we had to do a certain amount of drill. I was quite good at that but my friend Paddy (her real name was Patricia) definitely wasn't. She was a bit plump and, for some reason, she found marching difficult and one day the sergeant in charge singled her out and shouted at her. She burst into tears. So I broke ranks and put my arms round her. That was quite a serious breach of discipline, I suppose. But I didn't care.

Soon after that I was sent on an officer's training course, at the end of which we had to stand up and speak on any subject we liked for ten minutes. Girls talked on subjects as varied as 'How to Shampoo a Dog', 'What it was like Working in a Blanket Factory' and 'How I Managed to Escape from Russia after the Revolution', as told by a White Russian princess. Anyway, I was the very last to speak and I was so nervous I proceeded to talk about the first thing that came into my head for ten long minutes. I can't remember what it was now. But it can't have been too terrible because soon after that I was given a job teaching WAAF officers how to speak in public.

My next posting was to London, where I was in charge of recruiting. One of the young women who came into my office was a volunteer called Sarah Churchill, the Prime Minister's daughter. Girls like her often came in with their well-to-do parents and expected to be made officers and given a smart uniform the same day. I had to explain that it wasn't like that – they all had to start at the bottom as ACWs, even the Prime Minister's daughter.

My next posting was to an airfield in Northern Ireland – Castle Archdale. It was a Coastal Command Station by the side of a beautiful lough. It was a lively place, with parties and ENSA [Entertainments National Service Association] concerts almost every night. There were a lot of Canadians there and they were very generous with their tins of peaches – the RAF airmen always complained that they couldn't get a girl because they had no peaches to offer! The food there was much better because a lot of it came up from southern Ireland where there was no rationing.

Looking back on it, I'm very, very glad that I volunteered for the WAAFs. It changed my life hugely. In fact, I thought of girls who weren't in the services as wimps. I didn't mind the discipline – I learnt to break the rules occasionally. We all did. I was promoted quite rapidly and ended up squadron officer. The funny thing is, by this stage, part of my job was to discipline WAAFs who broke the rules with a week in the cookhouse or cancelled leave. Funny to think that only quite recently I'd been the one who'd been breaking the rules. I'd grown up fast.

To me, being in the WAAFs was an adventure. I made good friends with girls from all over the country and from different backgrounds – some had never had a bath before they joined up! But we bonded really well because we all had a common purpose.

That last comment could have been echoed by many, if not all of the women I spoke to who had served in one of the services during the war. Unlike conscripts in peacetime, women who were called up in wartime generally felt it was a hugely worthwhile and, in many cases, life-changing experience.

Another volunteer for the women's services was **Eve Cherry**. She made the brave decision, or perhaps the decision was made for her, to join the ATS. The chauvinists of the time dubbed the ATS 'the groundsheet of the army'. In fact, a Wartime Social Survey Report reflected the gross misogyny of the time when it commented:

The ATS appears to have been from the beginning the drab and unglamorous service, the legion of Cinderellas, domestic workers of low degree among whom one expected, and got, a low degree of morality. Men called them 'female Tommies' and even 'scum of the earth'. When girls register at Labour Exchanges and allow themselves to be indicated for a Service, their first stipulation is usually NOT the ATS.

But **Eve** did not allow this to deter her. She continued:

I was kitted out with a uniform which I remember didn't fit. In fact, there was only a very remote chance of it fitting because they just issued you with the next one on the pile, irrespective of how tall or slim you were.

An enterprising cosmetics manufacturer, Yardley, did its best to counter the blandness of the khaki uniform by developing a special new colour, which it advertised thus, 'If you have to stay in khaki, don't despair. There is a lovely new make-up created especially for you. Its name is Burnt Sugar. It is a warm, glowing shade that goes beautifully with your uniform.'

Eve particularly hated the rather shapeless brown hat that was part of the ATS uniform:

I hated wearing the hat I was issued with because I had beautiful hair and I didn't want to hide it. Anyway, when I was driving, my hat spent most of the time on the seat beside me, not on my head.

I was then sent to Camberley in Surrey and there we were allocated various jobs. I was adamant that I wanted to be a driver, which was odd really since I didn't have a driving licence. So I was given driving lessons – funnily enough, the future queen, Princess Elizabeth, was being given lessons at the same time although I never spoke to her. I wouldn't really have known what to say. And she certainly didn't share a wooden Nissen hut with twenty other girls – she was driven home every night to Windsor Castle.

I also had to spend one day a week in overalls learning basic mechanics, things like changing tyres, oil and spark plugs.

Eventually, I was posted to the Southern Command Blood Supply Unit. Basically, our job was to collect blood from donors all over the south of England. I drove around in a Bedford 3-ton lorry with a big red cross on the side. On board were two girls like me and a doctor – the 'bleeding team' as we were called – together with a supply of beds, stretchers, syringes and glass blood bottles. I drove us round to village halls and schools and then we used to take one pint of blood from every donor that came in. I then had to give them a cup of tea and a biscuit as they lay down on a stretcher on the floor to rest.

Men were by far the worst 'patients'. They would fidget and smoke to calm their nerves and in looking for their cigarettes or matches they would often dislodge the needles in their arms causing a terrible mess – and a waste of blood – and I was the one who had to clean up the mess! At the end of the day, we drove the blood we'd collected to Southmead Hospital in Bristol to be sent on to wherever it was needed. [For the conclusion of **Eve**'s story in the 'bleeding' team, see page 237.]

Rosemary Strydom was only 16 in 1940 so officially she was too young to join any of the services:

But I was desperate to join one of them. Unfortunately, the WAAFs and the Wrens wouldn't accept me without a birth certificate – I'd lost that and most of my clothes and personal possessions when our house in Pimlico was destroyed by a landmine. But luckily for me, the ATS gave me the chance to lie about my age – I told them I was 18.

After my initial training I was sent back to London, to Eaton Square in Belgravia to be exact, which by coincidence was quite close to where I came from and where my mother now lived. The ATS had requisitioned a big six-storey house in the square owned by the Duke of Westminster, a house which would nowadays be worth millions.

I shared a small room with another girl in the servants' quarters on the top floor. There were about twenty of us ATS girls in the house altogether and we all ate our meals in the big servants' kitchen in the basement. We came from all over the country and we all mucked in and got on really well.

Every morning I had to march to work in Birdcage Walk wearing my uniform with the Grenadier Guard badge pinned to the front of it. I was very proud of that badge. I worked normal office hours, doing shorthand and typing, and after work I used to go to the pub round the corner and Grenadier Guards used to join us, although I only used to drink shandy – I was still only 17.

I enjoyed my time there, but I wanted a bit more excitement in my life so I applied to go abroad. It was a very fateful decision, as it turned out. Soon after that, I was issued with a summer uniform so I knew it was going to be reasonably warm and then I caught a train to Liverpool and embarked with hundreds of others on a liner which had been converted to a troop ship. We were then told where we were going – southern Italy. On the way there, I remember we dropped a lot of depth charges to keep German submarines at a safe distance.

We landed in Naples – I was one of the very first ATS girls to land in Italy – and from there, I was sent to Rome in the back of an army lorry, sitting on hard, wooden benches. It was a long, bumpy and uncomfortable journey but we were welcomed by the Italians with open arms, despite the fact that we had, until recently, been fighting on opposite sides in the war. I remember, we drove past the site of the Battle of Monte Cassino and the destruction we saw on the way was terrible.

In Rome we were billeted in rooms near the centre of the city. I loved Rome. It was a beautiful city. And soon after I got there, by pure chance, I met up with my brother David. That was a wonderful surprise because we'd always been very close. He'd been fighting in North Africa and now he was fighting his way up through Italy. I was feeling a bit apprehensive, on my own in a foreign country – I'd never been abroad before – and for me to meet my own brother. It was such an incredible coincidence.

But there was one small problem. David was an officer by this time and of course, he invited me to join him in the Officers' Club to meet all his friends and celebrate the fact that he was still alive. But would you believe it, he got into trouble for inviting me in because I was only a private! [For a description of what happened next to **Rosemary Strydom**, see page 198.]

Brenda Gillingham (née Gimson) read mathematics at Oxford and then became a Wren:

I took my finals through the crisis of the Dunkirk evacuation and the Battle of Britain when defeat seemed a real possibility. I then got a job working for the Admiralty in Bath, as a statistician. I had to make sense of the huge volume of statistics relating to the Battle of the Atlantic, the number of convoys, the number of ships lost and so on. My summaries were then sent direct to Churchill in such a comprehensible and simplified form that even he, who was notoriously bad at maths, could understand them. I suppose, looking back on it, it was really quite important war work.

A year later, after I'd been reunited with my husband Anthony who was in the Fleet Air Arm [see page 189] and also a mathematician, my mathematical skills were used again to good effect. The Admiralty had asked us if we could produce a formula to find in what area a U-boat might attack the convoy within the next three hours. We sat up together for most of the night producing various equations, the variable being the speed of the convoy and the known constants being the maximum speed of the U-boat on the surface and submerged, and the distance from the convoy the U-boat would submerge for safety. Eventually, Anthony went to bed, leaving me to work out the final figures and diagrams. I finished them just before dawn.

Anthony's commander couldn't make head nor tail of what we'd done so Anthony had to explain it to him as best he could. He was delighted. And then, a year later, I saw 'my' equation and diagrams in an Admiralty publication for use with all convoy escorts. I got a lot of satisfaction out of that but no acknowledgement!

The other women's service, the WLA (Women's Land Army), was first started in 1939 to provide a labour force on farms which urgently needed replacements for their male workers who had gone off to join the armed services. By 1943, there were more than 80,000 women wearing the WLA uniform. **Valerie Hodge**, from Bristol, was one of the first to volunteer for the Land Army, despite the fact that she had absolutely no experience of agricultural work. Her call-up was used for publicity purposes when she was presented to King George VI. She said at the time, 'Here was the thing for me, the service to serve England, the service to keep this land alive and also the service in which I could help in the everlasting process of creation instead of helping in destruction.'

The WLA training manual made it clear that it wasn't glamorous work, 'The WLA volunteer should be prepared to tone down her lips, complexion and nails considerably. Long nails are quite unsuited to work on a farm, especially when covered with bright crimson nail varnish.'

And it wasn't easy work that they were being asked to do. A working week of fifty hours was compulsory and many women worked far longer hours, particularly at harvest time. And while the recruiting posters might have had pictures of smiling girls bottle-feeding pet lambs, the reality included digging, haymaking, potato-picking, milking, muck-raking, ditch-clearing, tractor-driving, hedging, weeding, baling, calving, castrating lambs and rat-catching. In fact, just the sort of dirty, back-breaking jobs that farmers were more than happy to give these badly paid but willing workers.

Enid King's experiences in the WLA could be described as mixed:

In 1940, I was working on the sweet counter at Woolworth's which paid quite well but wasn't exactly war work. So I decided to volunteer for the WLA instead.

I was given a uniform which consisted of dungarees and Wellington boots, a pair of jodhpurs, a fawn-coloured shirt and a green V-necked jumper, an overcoat and a sort of pork-pie hat. Many girls added to the uniform with two or three old sacks which they tied round their waist with baler twine.

I was sent to a farm just outside Bristol. The farmer was a man called Mr James. He seemed to think he was a bit of a gentleman farmer and he didn't like to get his hands dirty. His attitude was, 'You're here to do a man's job so just get on with it.'

He had a large herd of Friesian cows and they had to be milked twice a day. Fortunately, Mr James had installed a milking parlour so his cows didn't have to be milked by hand. One of my first jobs was to get those cows in for milking. That wasn't too difficult. But then the hard work started. After milking I had to fill hundreds of milk bottles with milk and put them all in crates. Then I had to help Mr James with his milk round. I did most of the work – he just sat in his van while I got the bottles of milk off the back, took them to the doorsteps and brought back the empties.

Mr James kept pigs too and another of my jobs was mucking out the pig sties. It was hard, smelly work, so Mr James certainly didn't help me with that either.

But a job I did enjoy was hay-making. We used to do it late into the evening, sometimes as late as midnight. I drove the tractor that pulled the hay wagon and then I used a pitchfork to heave the bales onto the wagon. It was easy at first but got more and more difficult as the pile of bales got higher.

Myrtle Young also described her work as a Land Girl, which was similar in many ways to **Enid King**'s:

I worked on a mixed farm with dairy shorthorn cows, pigs, sheep and hens and I was responsible for milking forty cows. They were lovely animals, I remember. And we had a wonderful bull called Joe. He was very big but with me he was very docile, as good as gold, like a kitten. With men, though, he could be very dangerous. I think he hated men and they told me his grandfather had killed a man.

I worked very hard. I had to be up early, before 6 a.m., to do the milking and by the time I'd finished the afternoon milking it was 6.30 p.m. And I only had one weekend off a month! But I was young and energetic and I was helping to feed the people of our country and so win the war!

Almost all of the women I spoke to who volunteered or were conscripted into the services experienced a completely new way of life, and one of them was lucky enough to be posted to newly liberated Rome where her whole life was to change. There were disadvantages to wearing a uniform – it seldom fitted and it was anything but glamorous – but the services provided the women with new friends, very close friends, in new places. It also taught them different skills and gave them hugely expanded horizons.

7

War Work

With men in short supply as a result of conscription, more and more women were employed to do what were traditionally regarded as men's jobs and were effectively 'called up'. Put simply, Britain's labour and industrial resources had to be mobilised as rapidly as possible and that necessitated the conscription of women. In March 1941, an Act of Parliament required all women over the age of 20 to register for war work of some sort, no matter that they had been brought up to believe that their rightful place was in the home.

Eventually, the net was widened, and by 1943, 90 per cent of single women and 80 per cent of married women were employed in some form of war work. The repercussions were enormous. In May 1941, a radio talk included the following stirring plea, 'Today, we are calling all women. Every woman in the country is needed to pull her weight to the utmost ... We are fighting for our lives – for our freedom and our future.'

Very soon, the whole attitude of women to work changed radically. Men also had to accept the fact that their sisters, girlfriends and wives were actually going to work, outside the home, and earning money. It came as a big shock to many of them. The cage door had well and truly opened, and millions of the so-called 'weaker sex' were now doing 'men's work'.

One telling example of how women were propelled into new roles was the use of women pilots to fly newly manufactured or repaired aircraft from factories to aerodromes all over the country. An editorial in the *Aeroplane* magazine in 1940 thundered, 'The menace is the woman who thinks she ought to be flying a high-speed bomber when she really has not the intelligence to scrub the floor of a hospital.' In the face of such outrageous contempt for women, it was something of a triumph that 168 women, members of the ATA (Air Transport Auxiliary), piloted over 100 different types of aircraft without any communication with the ground and only maps with which to navigate. By so doing, they totally disproved the antediluvian editor of the *Aeroplane*.

Theoretically, women were free to choose whether to join one of the armed services, work in an office or in a factory. In practice, the laws of supply and demand dictated that most ended up working in factories, whether they liked it or not. Many were reluctant because it was often hard, dirty and sometimes dangerous.

By 1943, 47 per cent of the industrial workforce was made up of married women and a third of those had children – in some cases, many children. This so-called Battle for Production had dramatic results. During the war, up to 40 per cent of the workers in the aircraft industry, 52 per cent of those in the chemical and explosives industries and, perhaps most surprisingly, 33 per cent of those in shipbuilding and heavy engineering were women. They produced anything from aircraft engines to shells, ships to guns, and uniforms to tanks.

There was a problem, though. Many women resented the fact that they were paid much less than men doing the same job. So much so, that in one Glasgow factory which was making 400 Rolls-Royce Merlin engines a week for Spitfires and Hurricanes, skilled women machine operators were paid £2.15 a week, whereas men got £3.65. So 16,000 employees, led by a redoubtable woman, Agnes McLean, went on strike. As a result, women got a sizeable pay increase, although they still earned less than the men in the factory.

Most unpopular of all the factory jobs was working in munitions. Around 950,000 British women worked in munitions factories during the war. It was relatively well paid but it was also heavy, dangerous work. Most munitions workers handled toxic chemicals every day. Those who handled sulphur were nicknamed 'canary girls' because their skin and hair turned yellow from con-tact with the chemical.

One munitions worker, **Gwen Thomas**, from Liverpool, described what it was like (her story is featured in the Liverpool Museum):

There was no training. You were just put into what they called small shops where they made different sizes of shell and landmines and different things like that. You were just told what you had to do, filling them with TNT.

It was quite heavy work actually, because they used to have a big cement-mixer type of thing and this was full of hot TNT. The smell was terrible and you had to go to that with something like a watering can. Then there was a chap on it who used to tilt it and fill your can and you'd have to carry that to where you were working and then fill the shells from the can.

I slipped on the floor once with one of those big cans and I was covered in TNT. My eyes were completely covered, I remember, and everything went up my nose. It was everywhere. So then some of the chaps who were working there got hold of me and put me onto a trolley and took me down to the medical place and then I just had to wait for it to set on my face. I remember I had a terrible job getting it off my eyelashes and, of course, my face then was all red and scarred with the hot TNT so they put me on a bed for an hour or so. But then it was straight back to work after that!

It was dangerous work because there was always the risk of an explosion caused by a rogue spark. **Irene Booker**, who started work on her eighteenth birthday at the Rotherwas Munitions Factory in Herefordshire, remembers having to strip down to her underwear to be inspected before she was allowed to start work, 'You took everything off and if your bra had a metal clip on the back you couldn't wear it … and no hair grips, of course, because they would cause friction and explosions.' This super-cautious policy paid off. Of the 8,000 workers at the ordnance factory during the war, only three were killed in one accident. **Nellie Brook** helped to build Lancaster bombers:

I was told my services were needed at AV Roe at Yeadon near Leeds. That place was like something out of science fiction. To get there we were taken out by bus into the country. When you arrived, you would never have thought there was a factory there, it was so well camouflaged. But once you went inside, it was amazing. No windows, all these thousands of people of both sexes all working like ants, all doing different jobs that finished up producing one of Britain's finest planes.

Yeadon was close to what is nowadays Leeds Bradford Airport. It was a shadow factory built on a huge scale, covering approximately 34 acres or 1.5 million square feet. It was at the time the largest single factory unit in Europe. The factory was so well camouflaged and practically invisible from the air that no German bombers ever dropped a single bomb on it. This was just as well because when it was fully operational, 17,500 people, of whom **Nellie Brook** was just one, worked there. They worked very long hours: sixty-nine hours a week, three days followed by three nights. Workers were brought in from all over west Yorkshire in a fleet of 150 buses.

Having children did not in any way exempt women from doing war work. Of those I spoke to, most had to rely on their mothers to take over childcare while they were at work. **Iris Gillard**, for example, had a full-time job in the accounts department of a big company in Bristol:

> But I was obviously good at my job because, soon after that, they sent me to work in their head office in Commercial Road, London. That meant I had to leave my baby with my mother at home in Bristol and just travel home on the train at weekends to see my baby daughter. It was terribly difficult being separated from her, but it wasn't unusual in those days.

To some women, having to get a job came as a great shock. **Diana England**, in particular, described what it was like for an upper-class girl to be forced to work for the first time in her life. Before she volunteered for the WAAFs (see page 114), she got a job:

> My mother decided to send me away to a Domestic Science College in Dorset. There I learned how to iron and clean a room and cook things like white sauce and how to do the fires. At home, of course, we'd always had servants to do all these things for us, so clearly I had a lot to learn in a very short time. But I did learn and matron once said, 'If Diana has cleaned a room, you know it's really been cleaned properly!'
>
> I did that job for nearly two years, but in all that time I was only allowed to use the back stairs because I was only a servant after all. But I enjoyed it because it was war work and I really thought I was doing my bit. After that I worked at a convalescent home for other ranks. Apart from our servants, I had never met 'other ranks' before. But I just got on with it. I cleaned, dusted and swept the floors and I helped serve the men's meals, or at least I spooned the food out of an enormous container onto their plates.
>
> Many of the wounded men had fought in France and been evacuated from Dunkirk. I talked to them a lot, although I wasn't a nurse, only a cleaner, so I didn't wear a uniform, only an apron.

Elizabeth Longney came from a similar social background to Diana and for the duration of the war, she had a responsible and occasionally dangerous job:

> When I was 17, I was drafted into the GPO [General Post Office] to do war work as a telephonist. I got the job partly because of my voice – I've always

had a very clear speaking voice. I worked at the big exchange right in the centre of the city. That may not sound like difficult or dangerous work but that particular telephone exchange was in an area which was repeatedly targeted by German bombers and my job was to put through many of the emergency calls made during air raids.

I worked on the switchboard and I worked shifts, usually from 8 a.m. till 4 p.m., 9 a.m. till 5 p.m. or 10 a.m. till 6 p.m. We only had a ten-minute coffee break in the middle of the morning and then half an hour for lunch, although by the time you'd walked across the yard to the canteen and then queued you didn't have more than a few minutes to actually eat your lunch. I've eaten fast ever since!

There were hundreds of girls working there, from all over Bristol, and I remember once I asked one of them where she lived. 'Whitehall,' she answered. I was very surprised that she travelled down from central London every day to work and I didn't find out till later that Whitehall was then a poor district of Bristol which I'd never even heard of.

The worst shift was the one from 4 in the afternoon till 11 at night because that meant walking home in the dark in the middle of the blackout. I used to walk with my head down as fast as possible. On those days, I used to wear trousers so I looked more like a man than a girl so I was less likely to be attacked.

One of my jobs was to time every call I put through and then, when they finished, make a note of the cost. I remember, even now, that a three-minute call to London cost 3/-, which was a lot of money in those days. I quite enjoyed the work because nothing was automatic. I had to talk to real people.

I wasn't well paid. I only got £3 a week and I had to give my mother half a crown, a sizeable part of my wages, towards my board and lodging. I suppose I could have applied to be a supervisor – they were much better paid – but that would have meant standing around all the time instead of sitting and I really didn't fancy that idea.

Of course, we weren't meant to listen in to phone calls once we'd made the connection. And anyway, like most phone calls, they would have been very banal. But I do remember, one Sunday afternoon I put a call through from Princess Elizabeth in Buckingham Palace to a young naval lieutenant who was stationed at the time just outside Bath. I was sorely tempted to listen in but, in fact, I only heard the beginning of the conversation, and I can't tell you what they said because I suppose I'm still bound by the

Official Secrets Act. It wasn't very interesting though. The young man later became Prince Philip.

Margaret Walton, like most of the women I interviewed, left school when she was only 14 and got a job immediately. In her case, she worked in a green-grocer's shop. But she was clearly destined for more interesting work:

After working there for about six months I got a job at the Grand Spa Hotel in Bristol, as the post girl, sorting out all the letters that arrived. I got almost double the wage I was getting at the greengrocer's. Then, after two months, I told the manageress I wanted something more interesting. 'So where do you think you'd be better off?' she asked me. And I said, 'In Flying Control.'

The Grand Spa Hotel at the time was the head office of BOAC [British Overseas Airways Corporation], which was the only civilian airline in the country. Anyway, I was rewarded for my cheek. I got a job arranging the flying rotas of all the BOAC pilots. That was much more interesting.

After working there for some time, I was moved to the BOAC offices out at Whitchurch Airfield. In those days, I think it was the only civilian airport left in the country and we used to have regular flights to Lisbon and Shannon, en route to America. The flights to Portugal were never shot down by the Germans although they often had British agents on board. It turned out later that many German agents came into Britain on the return flights and that's perhaps why.

Dorothy Bailey was born in 1925 and worked at the Bristol Beaufighter factory at Oldmixon, Somerset. The Bristol Aeroplane Company had moved part of its production to shadow factories away from Filton, which had been badly bombed in 1940 (see page 78). **Dorothy** made these notes, explaining exactly what her job involved:

I worked in a flight shed where Beaufighters were at the last stage before flying. I fixed the pilot's compass on the left-hand side of him and a metal stand, the 4BA bolt. I had to put in the four corners, then underneath the stand had a nut on top of my finger and screw the two together. It was easier doing the one for the gunner. He also had two instruments on a panel above his head.

The pilot had a Blind Flying Panel, which was a flat piece of metal about 12 x 9 with all his six instruments fixed in it. It would be facing him after being fixed in, and there was an Aloa Pipe going from front to back. Sometimes it got damaged by others putting in their work, usually the radio. I would go along the pipe with a small cone of water, soap and a brush to find out where the bubbles were, then replace that part. The Petter Head was at the far end of the wing for getting the air through. I had to put my mouth around this pipe and blow air in or suck it out to test which way the instruments were going.

This description illustrates how often complex and highly skilled jobs on military aircraft, usually comprehensible only to trained aeronautical engineers, were undertaken by often poorly educated women as young as 18.

Kathleen Gates left school in 1937 and started work almost immediately:

I was only 14 but I got a job making packets for Wills Cigarettes, cigarettes like Woodbines and Gold Flake. It wasn't really war work. But after that I got a very different job. When I was 16, I went to work for a big engineering company called Lysaghts. I used to do electric welding of iron parts which were used for the building of Bailey Bridges and things like that. And then I had a baby. But that didn't stop me from working, not for long at least. As soon as I was able, I was back to work, leaving my baby with my mother.

Margaret Wells also left school at the age of 14 and soon got a job in a factory, but in her case it was the Bristol Aircraft Company:

I was just a slip of a girl but I was trained to be a fitter's mate, making the Bristol Beaufighter. I never thought I'd do all the things I did there, like welding, drilling and swinging things around. In fact, there wasn't much I didn't do on the 'benches', as they used to call them.

Rosemary Baker was only 10 when her father died of bronchitis in 1940 – he'd been gassed in the First World War:

This meant that my mother could no longer just be a 'housewife' but had to get out and find a job as soon as possible. She became a Red Cross welfare officer and she had to travel all over Nottinghamshire looking after people with all sorts of problems and she often had to work nights. I was left on my own at home for a lot of the war. So I got a job of sorts – I became the cook and housewife for the two of us. My mother used to leave me our ration books and shopping lists and it was my job to plan, shop and cook most of our meals. And I was only a young girl!

Rosemary Baker.

Dorothy Kears chose to put herself in harm's way when it came to war work:

After two or three years working for Wills, I got a job in the timekeeper's office at the Bristol Aeroplane Factory in Filton. The office was right in the middle of the factory floor where they were making aircraft at all hours of the day and night. It was quite dangerous work because the factory was attacked several times by German bombers, sometimes without warning. At times, we seemed to be constantly running to the shelters and on one occasion, several girls were caught running to the shelter by German aircraft and shot as they were running. That was dreadful. [For another account of this raid, see page 78.]

Ruby Spragg was one of seven children living in a small, terraced house in central Bristol:

At school I was bright, but as soon as I was 14 my parents told me it was time to leave school and get a job. I remember I cried because I loved school and I loved learning. But with so many mouths to feed, someone over the age of 14 and not working was a luxury they simply couldn't afford. Anyway, after I'd worked at Wills for four years, hating almost every minute of it, I decided to do something more like real war work, a man's job. So in 1942, when I was 19, I got a job on the railways.

I worked in the goods yards at Temple Meads station. It was very big in those days, with fifteen platforms. Long trains with truck load after truck load of goods used to come in from all over the country. Our checker, an older man called George Turner — a nice man he was — then had to look at all the labels and assign them to us to take to different trains for transport on from there — very little went by road in those days. Before long, I had a truck load which was usually very heavy to take to a different platform to be put onto a different train to be transported to wherever.

I worked in a gang of six girls and young women and we got to know each other ever so well. We used to talk and work at the same time. A lot of talk was about the Americans, after they arrived in Bristol. The girls took a lot of interest in them.

Our basic wage wasn't very good but the more trucks we emptied and the greater the tonnage we moved the more we got paid, so we worked fast. Sometimes we even worked on Sundays, when we got time and a half, and that meant I was working a seven-day week. I reckon I used to walk, with a heavy load on my truck, between 15 and 20 miles a day.

Yes, it was hard, tiring work but we were working in the open, although in winter it was bitterly cold. I sometimes used to wear my pyjama trousers underneath my overalls to try and keep warm. But there was a war on and I think I enjoyed it. It was a friendly place to work and we were well paid. I got £4 or £5 a week, which really was a lot of money in those days, especially for a girl. But we earned it.

It's difficult to generalise, but most of the jobs undertaken by women were demanding, arduous and sometimes dangerous and for which they were initially unqualified or unsuited. But very few complained. They just got on with it because there was a war on. The pity of it is that after the war, most women discovered that they had only been let out of the cage on temporary licence.

Teachers, doctors and students didn't have it easy either. Their jobs were also radically affected by the

Ruby Spragg, who worked for most of the war loading and unloading trucks at Bristol Temple Meads station.

war. **Phyllis Edwards** was a University of Bristol student during the Blitz but she also had a part-time job as a firewatcher:

> We trained for this in some big, long sheds that had been specially erected in the garden of our hall of residence. We had to crawl on our hands and knees from one end to the other of a smoke-filled shed, wearing gas masks and keeping our noses less than 8in from the ground, where it was said the air was fresher.
>
> After that, we had to learn the inside layout of the buildings that we were protecting, in the blackout by torchlight only. That involved counting the number of steps and then climbing up ladders in the dark and then out onto the roofs of our hall of residence. It wasn't easy.

Rose Jennings was a student at the beginning of the war but then got her first job as a PE teacher at a girls' school in Bristol:

> The job was far from straightforward. During the bombing raids, I was on fire watching duty twice a week. I spent the night in the staff room at school with two other teachers. I must admit I took catnaps on the sofa but we couldn't really go to sleep, although that was difficult because I'd already had a normal working day, teaching. But I still had to go to work the next day as normal. Life was hard during wartime but we all had to do our bit.
>
> Another difficult thing about my job was the shortage of equipment. I had just three netballs and three tennis balls and I used to have to count them in at the end of every lesson. At the end of the first term, I was exhausted.
>
> But then I was also required to work during my long summer holidays. I used to take the girls from our school potato-picking down in Cornwall. We used to sleep under canvas and Italian prisoners of war used to dig our latrines and do the washing up for us. That caused problems sometimes. One girl ran off with an Italian prisoner when we were in Cornwall.
>
> I also had to lead by example and it was extremely hard work. We had to fill buckets full of potatoes and take them to sacks at the end of the row. We worked from 9 a.m. till 5 p.m. with only an hour off for lunch. And my work didn't really stop at 5 p.m. either. I was never really free. In the evenings I used to organise games, things like treasure hunts, and we sang songs.

Looking back on it now, I suppose it was a kind of war work we were doing. Someone had to pick those potatoes and we were cheap labour – the farmer didn't have to pay the girls at all, only provide their food.

In 1942, when **Rose Jennings** was down in the south-west of England picking potatoes, she might just have met **Mildred Lovejoy**, who at the time was a second-year biology student at the University of Bristol. **Mildred** described her job that summer:

About Easter we were visited by an official from the Ministry of Agriculture who interviewed all biology students for jobs on farms in the summer holiday. They wanted students to inspect potato crops in the west of England for Colorado beetles which they said were being blown over from France. Normally, very few potatoes are grown in Devon and Cornwall, although a lot in the Channel Islands, but unfortunately they'd been invaded by the Germans. So now all farmers in the west country were expected to give up at least 25 per cent of their land to potato-growing. [The total area used for potato-growing increased by 92 per cent, compared to pre-war levels.]

As biologists, we were expected to know exactly what a Colorado beetle looked like and their caterpillars and pupae. We were also expected to know the way the leaves are eaten to distinguish them from other beetles. None of that was part of our normal biology lectures so we had to learn fast.

Our job was to inspect about 15–20 acres a day, walking up and down every fourth row, looking left and right. So we walked many miles a day and on top of that we cycled many miles a day to and from the camp site where we lived. It was exhausting!

Like **Rose Jennings**, **Enid Beebee**, from Redruth in Cornwall, was also a teacher, a job you might think would be the same in wartime as in peacetime. Not so, it turned out:

My first job was in a small primary school, 3 miles away from Redruth, on the north Cornish coast. Unfortunately, the school buildings were in a terrible state of disrepair – the school had been closed down years ago. But with all the evacuee children arriving from London there was simply no room in the normal village school.

So what was wrong with this old school? Everything. The toilets were earth closets at the end of the playground. There was no electricity and no telephone and water came from a rusty old rainwater tank at the back of the school. For heating in my classroom we only had one very small stove which I, as the teacher, had to keep feeding with coal. To make matters much worse, having no electricity meant there was no lighting and the grills which they'd stuck over the windows to prevent flying glass shut out a lot of the natural light.

For lunch, many of the children used to have pasties – we were in Cornwall after all – and we used to heat them up in an oven at the side of the stove. If the oven became too hot the pasties would be burnt. Then, after lunch, if the children were quiet enough they watched fascinated as a family of mice used to come out and eat up the crumbs from the pasties. That was the only time there was ever complete silence in my classroom!

There was one other, major problem with that school – it was very near an aerodrome, RAF Portreath, with four concrete runways used at all times of the day by Spitfires, Beaufighters and bigger transport aircraft. With planes constantly landing and taking off, it was often impossible for me to teach – it was so noisy.

It was also quite dangerous at that school. In fact, one plane crashed less than 100 yards away and all the children in the school grabbed as many souvenirs as they could find. One boy found a live bullet and was heard saying to his friends, 'I wonder what would happen if I put this bullet on the fire!' An RAF man came round later that day and demanded they give them all back, including the bullet.

On another occasion two planes collided in the air near the aerodrome and debris was scattered over a huge area near the school. But it was all kept secret – nothing about the accident ever appeared in the local paper.

And then there was always the risk that the airfield would be attacked by German bombers. In fact, it was a totally unsuitable place to have a school! And the irony was that those evacuee children in 'my' school had been sent all the way down from London to be out of danger.

Apart from teachers, other jobs in the so-called 'professions' were also profoundly affected by the war. **Dr Mary Jones**, for example, described how she started work as soon as she was qualified:

When I passed my final exams in January 1944, I was immediately conscripted into the RAMC [Royal Army Medical Corps]. My job initially was to do FFIs on the men who were going to be sent off to fight in France.

I also inspected the girls who were being drafted into the ATS. I had to give them a very thorough physical examination – their hearts, lungs, eyes, feet, backs and so on. I was surprised how many of those girls were pregnant, although they themselves professed not to know it. One of the orderlies I worked with had the uncanny ability of smelling a pregnancy a mile away. When this happened, we simply sent for their mothers to take them home.

I was also responsible for the medical welfare of the prisoners in two prisoner-of-war camps. One was for Germans at Bower Ashton, about a mile from the centre of Bristol. It was quite intimidating entering that camp. I had a lot of respect for the German medical officer. He was very smart and efficient and could cope with most of the prisoners' problems. I simply had to countersign what he had prescribed.

The German prisoners were separated into three categories. Most were deemed to be more or less apolitical. They were conscripts but were indifferent to the ideology of the Nazi Party and wore white patches on their prison uniform. Then there were those who demonstrated some interest in politics and had a half-hearted loyalty to the Nazi Party. They wore grey patches. Finally, there were those, usually members of the Waffen SS, who were hardcore Nazis and unwavering in their absolute loyalty to Hitler and all that he stood for. They wore black patches and were usually segregated from the other prisoners. But I had to treat all three categories equally. I found it difficult sometimes.

I spoke a bit of German – I had learned it at school – but I found the attitude of some of the German prisoners very negative and resentful. I suppose they realised they were losing the war and they must have been bored to tears down there.

I also worked at another POW camp in Yate [a small town 12 miles from Bristol]. This was for Italian prisoners and the contrast could hardly have been more marked. They were, for the most part, charming and delightful. I suppose they were just happy to be out of the war and not required to fight. And I'll always remember that I was given the most gorgeous coffee when I visited that camp. I have no idea where they got it from and I didn't ask!

Pam Allcock told me about her parents and, in particular, her mother. Her father was a vet but was badly injured in a bombing raid (see page 101), which meant that her mother had to take over the running of her husband's veterinary practice to a large extent. **Pam** described what this involved:

While my father was recovering from his injuries, my mother became something of a heroine. She took it upon herself to find a locum to take over my father's practice and she then acted as receptionist, secretary and kennel maid, as well as looking after us two and visiting my father in hospital.

Dogs were tied to every chair and cats were accommodated in an old caravan in the garden. I remember our house at the time stank of the meat, probably most of it horse meat and offal, which was constantly on the boil in our kitchen to feed the animals. She also did fire watching two nights a week, worked in an emergency telephone exchange, joined the WVS and helped to run a canteen for soldiers camped out on the Downs. And she was also a full-time teacher.

She was a tremendously energetic woman, my mother!

Nearly all jobs were affected by the war. And the women who did them worked with enthusiasm and great energy. They, like all the women in this book, were expected to do much more, to cope with the unexpected and work way beyond the call of duty. But they did so without complaining.

Women at work making Spitfire fuselages in a factory in Birmingham. (Birmingham Museums Trust)

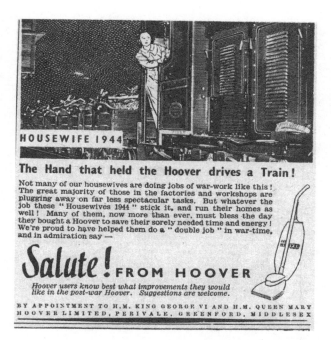

Two advertisements which illustrate how the roles of women changed completely during the war. (*Picture Post*)

Ration Book – essential if you wanted to eat. (iStock/chrisdorney)

8

Hard Times

Food Rationing

At the beginning of the war, Britain had a problem. As a country we were hugely dependent on imported food. For example, 70 per cent of cheese and sugar, 80 per cent of fruit and 70 per cent of cereals and fats all came from abroad. Only potatoes and fresh milk were produced entirely at home. The German High Command were obviously aware of this – hence the Battle of the Atlantic in which German U-boats attempted to sink as many merchant ships as possible and so starve Britain into submission. They almost succeeded.

Knowing how vulnerable Britain was to this naval blockade, the Ministry of Food decided to reorganise the entire food industry so the country could be 'fed like an army'. The ministry was headed by 58-year-old Lord Woolton who, in a previous incarnation, had been Fred Marquis, a Mancunian businessman in charge of a chain of department stores. His ministry, employing over 50,000 civil servants by 1943, controlled the manufacture and distribution of virtually all foods.

Initially, rationing by raising prices helped to control consumption. But, for some people, money was no object. They could just carry on buying whatever they liked and as much as they liked. This resulted in considerable discontent and resentment.

So rationing by price was abandoned and replaced by strict food rationing. The government had difficulty persuading the British public that rationing was a good thing, and the *Daily Express* wasn't convinced. It fulminated, 'The public should revolt against the food rationing scheme ... There is no necessity for the trouble and expense of rationing.' The government countered with this message:

Rationing will prevent waste of food, increase our war effort, divide supplies equally. There will be ample supplies for 44½ million people but we must divide them fairly, everyone being treated alike. Your ration book assures you of your fair share. Rationing means there will be no uncertainty – and no queues.

This was a wildly optimistic claim but the government got its way.

The standard ration book was a dreary buff colour; the one for expectant mothers was green. Many pregnant unmarried women were reluctant to change the colour of their ration books, preferring to keep their 'condition' private. But the extra pregnancy entitlements included seven pints of milk a week plus up to four fresh eggs!

Food rationing came into force little by little – and then in a rush. **HJF** first mentioned the bureaucracy of rationing on 25 September 1939:

Daddy is out again on work for the National Registration. He meets with some very peculiar people who will not give him any particulars about themselves. One man said it was only the government's sly way of finding out all about him, and then making him do something he did not want to do. He mistrusted it was anything to do with food rationing and said that he would rather starve!

The 1939 'register' enabled ration cards and identity cards to be issued. It held the personal details of 41 million people. Only a handful of homeless people, criminals and conscription dodgers slipped through the net.

Dorothy Jones remembered this need for registration, 'We all just thought, right, there's a war on, and if we don't want some people to starve we'd better share what food there is out fairly – and if that means rationing then so be it'.

In January 1940, rationing restricted bacon to 4oz (115g), butter to 2oz (50g) and sugar to 12oz (340g) per person per week. Far worse was to follow. Meat rationing was also introduced but this was rationed by price rather than by weight, so the cheaper the cut, the more you could buy. The trouble was the British were notoriously keen on eating meat – not for nothing did the French refer to us as '*les rosbifs*' (the roast beefs). So meat eaters had to choose carefully. Fillet steak would almost empty your ration book but you could eat more or less as many pigs' brains, calves' heads, pigs' feet and cows' udders as you wanted.

Even Camp Coffee was difficult to obtain during
the year. The advertisement was therefore only
intended to maintain brand awareness. (*Picture Post*)

Three books you couldn't do without during the war.
(iStock/whitemay)

In time, bacon, ham and pork became exceedingly difficult to come by but were replaced, to some extent, by Spam. This was an American invention – GIs referred to it as 'ham that didn't pass its physical' – but the British came to love it and carried on eating it after the war.

The British need to eat meat resulted in such delicacies as squirrel soup and crow pie and rabbits became a prized source of meat, selling for 8*d* each.

Two Cambridge scientists and a panel of volunteers reported on the effects of food rationing on the nation's health. They subjected themselves to the following rigorous diet: per week they were allowed one egg, 1lb (450g) of meat, 4 oz (110g) of fish, ¼ pint (140ml) of milk, 4oz (110g) margarine, plus unlimited quantities of potatoes, vegetables and wholemeal bread. This diet foreshadowed what the vast majority of the population had to get by on during the war. They concluded that there was no measurable deterioration in the volunteers' health. The only downside was 'the remarkable increase of flatulence owing to the large amount of starch in the diet'. Another interesting finding was the fact that faeces increased in volume by up to 250 per cent.

After the war, studies confirmed that the health of the British people during the war was improved, infant mortality went down and life expectancy went up. So no matter how much people grumbled about food rationing it actually did them good.

The next bout of rationing was announced in July 1940. Tea, cooking fat, jam and cheese were now also rationed. The cheese ration, for example, was reduced to a pitiful 1oz (28g) per week. Jam was noticeably reduced in quality as well as quantity – it became very thin and watery. Eggs were now in desperately short supply – each adult was only allowed a miserly one egg a fortnight – and butter was replaced almost ubiquitously by 'marge'.

When it came to fish, the staple varieties like cod and haddock became exceedingly expensive and by 1941, the price of fish had shot up seventeen-fold. 'Exotic' fruits like oranges and bananas were practically unobtainable, at any price. Some wartime children thought that bananas didn't really exist – they were only fantasy foods – and when they finally became available again after the war, some children ate them skins and all.

With the dire shortage of food from abroad, people were exhorted to eat homegrown rather than imported produce. Potatoes were promoted in adverts everywhere, featuring a cartoon character called Potato Pete, who suggested dubious delicacies like potato soup, potato cakes and even potato sandwiches. A Ministry of Food announcement had this to say:

Spam, an American invention, became part of the British diet during and after the war. (*Picture Post*)

Potatoes help to protect you from illness. Potatoes give you warmth and energy. Potatoes are cheap and home-produced. So why stop at serving them just once a day? Have them twice, or even three times, for breakfast, dinner and supper.

And potatoes meant the whole potato, including the skin, hence this exhortatory ditty:

Those who have the will to win,
Cook potatoes in their skin,
Knowing that the sight of peelings,
Deeply hurts Lord Woolston's feelings.

Carrots, because they were cheap and easy to grow, were also promoted with the claim that they helped you to see in the dark. This was scientifically complete baloney. In fact, Lord Woolton's claim that 'A carrot a day keeps the blackout at bay' prompted a *New York Times* journalist to write, 'To hear him talk, carrots contain enough Vitamin A to make moles see in a coal mine.'

There was one fruit, however, which was genuinely good for the nation's health – the humble prune or dried plum. The so-called 'Radio Doctor' repeatedly recommended the 'humble black worker', as he called it, 'to keep you regular'.

In April 1942, the 'national loaf' was first introduced. Unfortunately, it was a dirty grey colour rather than the far more popular white. In fact, white bread was dubbed 'Hitler's Secret Weapon'. In a similar way, the variety of cheeses was drastically reduced and replaced by the solid and uninspiring 'Government Cheddar'.

People were also exhorted to eat everything on their plate – 'Food wasted is another ship lost!' and the slogan 'A Clear Plate Means a Clear Conscience'.

When it came to methods of cooking, the Ministry of Food had yet more recommendations. Casseroles, or 'one-pot meals', became almost patriotic, promoted with the catchy slogan, 'Better pot-luck with Churchill today than humble-pie under Hitler tomorrow'.

Almost all the women I spoke to referred over and over again to food shortages. Rationing was obviously fairer but it didn't mean that shopping for food was straightforward or problem-free. **Vera Bartlett**, on her own for most of the war with two small children, said:

I had to get us something to eat. Rations didn't go far and shopping usually meant standing in queues for whatever was available that day. Often it was a question of joining the back of the queue and asking, 'What have they got today then?' You couldn't risk not getting whatever was available because it might not come back again.

Strangely, some things were in very short supply but others were freely available. You could usually buy carrots, potatoes and swedes, but for some reason onions were often impossible to get hold of. I used to love onions and I really missed them.

Rosemary Baker was a 10-year-old girl who was left to fend for herself for a lot of the war while her widowed mother worked. She was very capable but got things wrong sometimes:

One afternoon I came home from school starving hungry so I went to the larder and found some custard powder, dried milk and sugar which I made into a delicious custard pudding. My mother was furious – I'd used up our entire ration for that week for those ingredients.

HJF had plenty to say in her diary about rationing and food shopping:

8 January 1940: Rationing of bacon, sugar and butter begin today. When having tea in Boots Cafe we were only given four lumps of sugar – two each!

By this time, meat rationing was also becoming stricter too, although **HJF** didn't seem to notice:

9 September 1940: Several air raid warnings. I cooked a fowl and some roast pork for dinner, with carrots from our garden.

With stricter meat rationing, **HJF** spent a lot more of her time and energy planning meals:

2 April 1941: A shilling's worth of meat cuttings for dinner! Only two books of meat left for the week-end joint, as 1/- is the full allowance for the week for each person.

By this time, petrol rationing was at last limiting **HJF**'s trips into the countryside to buy three eggs – one for her, one for Daddy and one for Jean.

HJF's diary entry of Christmas Day, 1941 proves that, for some people, it was still possible to have a Christmas dinner despite rationing, 'Jean gave me three pairs of stockings, dear girl, out of her Christmas money from Mater. Lovely turkey, Christmas pudding and a bottle of white wine.'

But six months later, it's clear that her family's diet had become severely restricted:

6 June 1942: Opened a tin of tomatoes (6 points) on toast for supper.

On 20 July, their meagre diet was having unexpected consequences:

Daddy lost his gold ring and I found it embedded in the soap on the draining board in the kitchen. This is a sign of how thin he has become as the ring slips off his finger so easily.

And it wasn't just food that was in short supply – so were the means of carrying it:

13 February 1942: Bought three balls of macrame twine to make string bags to carry the shopping as wrapping paper and baskets have disappeared and paper bags and carriers are unobtainable.

Nevertheless, **HJF** was still able to send her daughter Jean a selection of things to eat after she'd gone away to college:

14 November: Packed a biscuit tin for Jean with 4lbs apples, biscuits, bloater paste and a tin of cycle oil for which she particularly asked, also a pot of peanut butter.

21 June 1943: Sent Jean two tins of beans in tomato sauce.

Vera Bartlett described how it wasn't just food that was in short supply:

Washing up was difficult because we couldn't get scrapers or scourers or cleaning materials, apart from Vim and soda which made my hands very red and sore. Rubber gloves were unobtainable because rubber was needed for far more important things. Housework involved getting down on my hands and knees and washing and scrubbing all by hand.

What **Vera** didn't mention was how strict soap rationing became. As a result, American GIs arriving in Britain noticed how smelly many British people were – and that included the women, whom they were more likely to get close to. To try and get round the problem, girls were advised to pat under their armpits with bicarbonate of soda. It reportedly didn't help much.

Eleanor Frost also described the trials and tribulations of food rationing:

Two or three days a week, it is necessary for me to go and see what provisions can be found to break the monotony of rations. I take the ration books and the small trolley to go to Clifton keeping a look-out for dates and other fruit. Occasionally there are things like Chinese figs and if these things are not bought immediately the opportunity may not come again for weeks. So home and fairly jaded. It is two miles there and back. No car of course – it is laid up.

So even for a woman like **Eleanor**, with plenty of money to spend, times were hard simply because there was very little to spend it on.

Another aspect of rationing was the war against luxuries. On 16 November 1940 the *Daily Herald* inveighed, 'LUXURIES YOU MUST DO WITHOUT ... gloves, lace, furs, mattresses, corsets, carpets, linoleum, pottery, glass, ... office furniture ... cutlery, cameras, musical instruments, sports goods, toys, fountain pens, umbrellas ...' So cutlery and a mattress had become luxuries. These really were hard times.

Joan Watkins described the effects of strict food rationing:

I often remember being hungry. For a growing girl like me – I was only 13 but already quite chunky and large – there never seemed to be enough food on the table to fill me up. My younger brother, who was as skinny as a rake and didn't have half my appetite, was always given the same-sized helpings. That didn't seem fair to me.

Food rationing during the war was a subject of endless comments, opinions and complaints from the women I spoke to. One summed up the effects of food rationing thus, 'With an all but meatless, fatless, fruitless, cheese-less larder and limited fuel, no matter how inventive the cook, meals were bound to be monotonous, dull and often beastly.'

And a journalist after the war summed up the dreariness and hard work that was a woman's lot during the war, 'It was a time of small, dull, makeshift meals ... darkness and drabness and making do, the depressing, nerve-aching, never-ending need to be careful.'

SHORTAGES

Fuel

As the war progressed, more and more things became in short supply – not just food. Life for almost everyone, and women in particular, became harder and harder and almost all the women I spoke to referred, over and over again, to shortages of all sorts of things.

Kathleen Gates remarked:

As well as food rationing it was also becoming difficult to get hold of coal. I used to go down to the gas works at Eastville with a small handcart and hold the sack open while a man poured coal into it. We had just one fire in the house to keep us warm in winter and I was only allowed one bath a week, in a tub in front of the fire.

Some families, in desperation, used their gas ovens as a form of heating. They opened the oven door and then took it in turns to put their feet in the oven.

Audrey Stacey was also cold because of a shortage of coal:

The only form of heating in our house was a small coal fire and I always remember my father used to sometimes come home from work on the bus with his bag of tools and in that bag he managed to hide a big lump of coal which he got hold of from work.

During the war, every household was almost completely dependent on coal. Domestic heating was from coal fires, hot water was from coal-fired boilers or coppers and many people were still cooking on coal-fired kitchen ranges. So when the government rationed coal to 2.5 tons per household, per year, it was extremely bad news.

Petrol rationing was also introduced almost as soon as war was declared, on 8 September 1939. Even **HJF**, who at the beginning of the war seemed to drive her car regardless of petrol rationing, wrote on 12 March 1940, 'Bought a "Sun" lady's bicycle for £7 12*s* 9*d* which includes three-speed gears, bell and bag. Not being able to use the car much now I shall find my purchase useful for shopping.'

On 29 July 1940, she wrote, 'Called in at the Petroleum Office for 3 months' petrol coupons being 5 gallons [23 litres] a month'. **HJF** could therefore reckon to drive no more than 125 miles a month. And that was early on in the war. Petrol later became unobtainable, for private cars at least. (The author's own father was forced to put his beloved family Wolseley up on bricks for the duration of the war.) In fact, petrol rationing was taken so seriously that the hugely popular composer and songwriter, Ivor Novello, was imprisoned for a month for what the papers described as 'the misuse of petrol coupons' – he used his car to go home every night after the show.

In early 1942, petrol rationing was becoming more and more strict and **HJF** was forced to cut right down on the use of her car:

15 March: Lovely day with a warm wind. Out in car to say 'goodbye' to the Mendips as our petrol ration will not allow us to go that far. [Perhaps **HJF** was unaware of a regulation that stated if you put a sign up in your car window offering lifts you were entitled to extra petrol coupons.]

But retribution followed:

16 May: A policeman called and asked if we were still running our car. I did not know how to answer at first as we were warned not to divulge information to the supposed 'enemy forces'. But as he was in uniform and insistent I finally answered, 'Yes.' Now I fear I may have helped the wrong side. But how was I to know?

Finally, on 30 June, **HJF** wrote, 'End of week's holiday. Returned to Bristol at 11 a.m. and cooked a hot lunch at home. This is the last day we can drive our car for the duration of the war.'

Shortage of Accommodation
Hard times and shortages were also experienced by people, particularly women, who found it difficult to find somewhere to live or simply keep a

roof over their heads. It is a fact that, during the war, 34 million 'changes of address' were registered. The whole population of Britain became infinitely more mobile and, in particular, huge numbers of girls and women were forced to somehow find accommodation, if they could, in strange places, far from home and with total strangers.

Many house owners were often unwilling to offer accommodation to children, servicemen and women, civil servants, industrial workers or bombed-out families. But, however reluctant, they had to show willing. **HJF** lived in a big house in Bristol with bedrooms to spare so it's not surprising that in her diary on 22 September 1939, she wrote:

> A Government Billeting Office called and asked me to take in two government officials, just for bed and breakfast, with high tea at 6 p.m. The government, I am informed, will pay me 25/- a week for each of the men. Secretly, I do not want to have them, but I reluctantly agree.

Incredibly the saga of **HJF**'s spare bedrooms rumbled on for the next eighteen months or so. On 17 December 1941 she wrote, 'Another Billeting Officer called and asked if I would put up two factory girl trainees. Billeting Officers have come so often; the bedrooms have been reluctantly prepared yet they never turn up. I expect this will happen again.' That was billeting from **HJF**'s point of view. It was something she only agreed to reluctantly.

The parents of **Pam Allcock** were threatened with a similar problem. They also lived in a large house in the centre of Bristol:

> My mother, now that she had two empty bedrooms in our house, thought she might have to have eighteen soldiers billeted on her, nine to a room. So she offered to have two billetees from the BBC instead. The BBC at that time was being moved, partially at least, from London to Bristol. One was a librarian at the BBC and the other a violinist in the Charles Shadwell Variety Orchestra. His name was Bernard Tigh and he'd had polio as a child, which was the reason he hadn't been called up.

A librarian and a musician must have been far more welcome than eighteen soldiers.

Of all the women I spoke to, **Vera Bartlett**'s story was, in many ways, the most affecting and confirms how difficult it was to find accommodation during the war, particularly if you had children. Her husband Ted went off to fight in France with the BEF and was one of the very last to be evacuated, several days after the last ship left Dunkirk (see page 222). He returned to England, only to be moved around the country before being sent to Italy and then France to fight, again. So as **Vera** described it:

> I was more or less on my own for the rest of the war, effectively a single mother. It wasn't easy. The first flat I had was in south London and cost me a guinea a week, I remember. The worst of it was that it was up three flights of stairs, which involved a lot of fetching and carrying with all the equipment that babies need. What made matters worse was the threat of invasion. In fact, that threat was so serious we were told to pack all our valuables into one suitcase and be ready to move to a safer part of the country at only a few hours' notice. I worried then how I was going to get the baby plus the baby's clothes and all his nappies into one suitcase and a carrycot. But, thank goodness, the invasion never came.

Sheila Kellard and her family were also bombed out of their house in Knowle, near the centre of Bristol, after a bomb scored a direct hit on their house:

> My parents decided that we couldn't go back and live in our house – it was too badly damaged. So sadly we had to salvage as much as possible of our furniture and move out to temporary accommodation in Nailsea [a small town approximately 5 miles from Bristol]. My mother was particularly upset to find that while our house was unoccupied, some looters got in and stole her jewellery. You wouldn't think people could stoop that low, would you?

Lorna McNab also experienced being bombed out of her family home, but in her case, she didn't have to travel far to find alternative accommodation:

> My mother was very resourceful and before long she went up and down Royal York Crescent in Clifton knocking on doors until eventually she found another more permanent flat for us on the top two floors of number 30. In a way, that bomb was the answer to my mother's prayers. Her in-laws couldn't carry on living with us!

Civilians who just needed accommodation, any accommodation, during the war were competing with bombed-out families and people who just wanted to get away from the bombing. In the winter of 1940, for example, the airlines BOAC and KLM had to move their entire operations out of Croydon Airport, which then became a key RAF base in the Battle of Britain. They moved to Bristol Airport, which was then located in Whitchurch, 4 miles outside the city. But what to do with all their staff?

For a time, they just had to put up with living in tents in a field next to the airport and being fed from hastily constructed field kitchens. The winter of 1940 was one of the coldest on record and those civilian employees must have really suffered until more suitable accommodation could be found for them. A local woman in Whitchurch offered them one small bedroom for rent – at a high price. She was then alarmed to find that *two* air hostesses were prepared to share the room and a single bed. One good thing resulted, however – when they moved on, the air hostesses left behind them two Imperial Airways wool blankets with 'IA, Croydon' embroidered in one corner. And woollen blankets in the war were in huge demand.

Peggy Turner had an extremely peripatetic war:

> As a newly married woman, the husband of an army officer, I was allowed to give up my job and then basically follow him round the country to every posting. And this incredibly amounted to twenty-two different places in the space of the next two-and-a-half years.
>
> I once made a list of all the places I lived in. They included: Cudworth, in Yorkshire, January 1941; High Wycombe, March and April 1941; Richmond, Yorkshire, 1941; Colchester, August and September 1941; Wix, in Essex, October 1941; St Osyth, Essex, October 1941; and so on and so on.

Keith, her husband, subsequently wrote an account of this miserable nomadic existence:

> Peg's letters NEVER whined, writing light-heartedly about sleeping in a cellar as though it was great fun, even when finding herself with a head full of lice was the result. It couldn't have been funny. I felt my sweetheart was bearing the brunt while her soldier husband was swanning around on Salisbury Plain.

Peggy continued her side of the story by rewinding to just before Christmas 1941:

I discovered I was pregnant and I went back to live in Woolaston, the village I came from in the Forest of Dean, before having our first daughter, Susan. She was born in July 1942 in Lydney Maternity Hospital. Keith managed to arrive soon after the birth but unfortunately on crutches – he had broken his ankle quite badly on exercises. [In his own words, 'I aroused the ire of the nurse when she took me in to see a sleeping Susan. Unfortunately, my crutches slipped on the polished floor, I grabbed a support and nearly put half a dozen baby-filled cots on the deck.']

Shortly after the birth of our daughter, Susan, I was back on the move again, this time to a very small labourer's cottage in Wiltshire. But it was very, very primitive, with no hot water and a toilet out the back, not ideal for a young mother and her new born baby. [The owners of the cottage were, according to Keith, 'one farthing short of a penny'.]

Another aspect of **Peggy**'s life at that time was the food she ate:

I remember while I was there I ate a lot of rabbit, presumably poached from the artillery ranges across the road. But somehow I coped – I had to. I saw Keith only infrequently. He was on duty most of the time on training exercises or doing administration. But just occasionally he was allowed to spend the night with us and I remember on those occasions, rather than eat his dinner in the Officers' Mess, he persuaded his batman, a middle-aged man called Private Liddell, to bring us our dinner, uncooked, and we heated it up on the old paraffin stove in the kitchen of the cottage. And although he had a wife and child of his own, it was Private Liddell, I remember, who looked after us when we were both in bed with flu. He also taught me how to cook.

Peggy then described in more detail her pillar-to-post existence:

Time after time, I used to pile everything we owned into a big trunk and what was left over into Susan's pram and set out, yet again, by train to somewhere completely new and unknown. The train journeys were often endless, with long delays because of bombs on the line or services withdrawn at the last minute for reasons unknown. Thank goodness every station had porters in those days, otherwise I would never have managed. But I was young and energetic and there were lots of other young mothers in the same situation as me, so there was absolutely no point in complaining. After all, there was a war on!

Peggy continued her description of places she lived in:

> This tiny cottage was eventually followed by the grandest house by far
> that we've ever lived in. It was called Boreham Manor, a huge eighteenth-
> century manor house with a big lake in front of it. We had a big room in
> the house with an open fire and Liddell had the unenviable job of bringing
> coal all the way up from the basement to burn on the fire to try and keep
> us warm.
>
> But we weren't there for long. Keith was soon on the move again and
> Susan and I followed. Keith always went on ahead to his new posting.
> Then, when he had time, he searched around the local area and contacted
> me to say what he'd managed to find. It can't have been easy. Lots of people
> were prepared to accommodate a young woman on her own but much
> more reluctant to have a mother and baby living with them, with all the
> crying and wet nappies that that involved.

Peggy summed up this period of her life, 'In those days, you just had to find
some sort of accommodation, in fact, anything that was available, however
small, cramped or unsuitable. It was a precarious, nomadic sort of life.'

★ ★ ★

To sum up the experience of living with shortages, **Vera Bartlett** said:

> There were so many shortages we just had to find a way round them. I even
> remember that at Christmas I wanted to decorate my Christmas tree but
> of course you couldn't buy 'luxuries' like Christmas decorations so I just
> had to make decorations out of milk bottle tops and the silver paper from
> empty cigarette packets. And the snow on the Christmas tree I made from
> cotton wool!

RECYCLING

Another aspect of the hard times that women experienced during the war was
the pressing need to recycle. **Eleanor Frost** wrote on 1 May 1940, 'At regular
intervals, we take parcels of bones, rags and also paper to the depot – bones
seem particularly acceptable.' On 16 February 1942, she mentioned recycling

bones again, 'I took bones to receptacles that smelt disgusting when their lids were removed.'

Bones were just one of the many things which the government urged people to recycle because of shortages of raw materials. They were boiled down to make glue used in the production of planes but also glycerine (an agent used in high explosives), soap, candles and crop fertiliser. One member of the WVS reportedly took her job so seriously that she dragged the entire skeleton of a horse to her car before dismantling it enough to fit in the boot.

Recycled materials and items were similar to today's, but during the war they included many more oddball items such as razor blades, rags, rope, string, rubber bands, cheque book stubs, bus tickets, old card games and jigsaw puzzles. The uses to which they could be put were as follows, 'One envelope makes 50 cartridge wads, 60 large cigarette packets make one outer shell container, one 9-inch enamelled saucepan makes a bayonet and a broken fork plus an enamelled pail makes a tommy gun', and so on. But most impressive of all, 'A mixture of leaky garden hoses, old rubber hot-water bottles, rubber teapot spouts, bathing caps and golf balls can be used to make barrage balloons and airmen's dinghies'.

In an effort to overcome shortages, nothing was spared it seems. Because paper was in short supply, public-spirited WVS Salvage Stewards encouraged people to recycle all their old or unread books. The campaign was so successful that by October 1943, 56 million books had been collected for pulping and recycling.

Other examples of the uses of recycled materials were as follows:

- Linen and calico could be used to make Admiralty charts
- Stiff white shirts and collars were transformed into £5 notes
- Knitted rags were used to make army uniforms
- Inferior-quality rags were used as mattress stuffing
- Scraps of any material could also be used to make roofing felt to help keep army huts less cold in winter.

And the campaigns worked. Everyone became extremely waste conscious. **Eleanor Frost** wrote on 20 February 1942:

Removed from my work basket this morning all the snippings of cotton and wool that I have dropped in there when sewing. I hear these 'national rags' at last emerge as heavy winter coats and blankets for the soldiers in the army.

There was another thing in short supply, which many women were very aware of – make-up. It wasn't rationed because it was said to be good for morale, but it was difficult to get hold of, partly because cosmetics firms switched their production to things that were really needed for the war effort. Coty, for example, famous for their face powders and perfumes, started producing army foot powder and anti-gas ointment instead.

Apart from the well-known use of gravy browning or boot polish applied to the legs ('liquid stockings', they called them), women went to great lengths to make up their faces with patriotic-sounding lipsticks like Yardley's 'Victory Red' and Helena Rubinstein's 'Regimental Red'. Such lipsticks were made even more attractive and longer lasting by a layer of petroleum jelly on the top. Other ways to get round shortages of make-up were the use of burnt cork or boot polish as mascara, beetroot juice for lipstick, bicarbonate of soda for a deodorant, lard or castor oil applied to the eyelashes to thicken them up and, most ingenious of all, burning the underside of a saucer with a candle and using the sooty residue as eye shadow.

As the war progressed, more and more things were recycled to overcome shortages. On 13 March 1942, **HJF** wrote, 'Mater complains that her garden railings and iron gate have been taken away by the government employees for munitions.' It turned out this was more of a propaganda exercise than anything. It's never been proved that these iron railings were ever used for anything like munitions.

Similarly, aluminium saucepans, pots and pans were collected religiously, in the belief that they would be transformed into Spitfires. This may or may not have been true. Housewives were exhorted to 'Send your Pans Flying!' This was followed by some rather dubious statistics: '5,000 make a fighter. 25,000 make a bomber'.

Lord Beaverbrook, Minister of Aircraft Production, added more detail in a press appeal on 10 July 1940:

We will turn your pots and pans into Spitfires and Hurricanes, Blenheims and Wellingtons ... Everyone that has pots and pans, kettles, vacuum cleaners, hat pegs, coat hangers, shoe trees, bathroom fittings and household ornaments, cigarette boxes, in fact any article made wholly or in part of aluminium should hand them over at once to the local Women's Voluntary Service ... The need is instant, the call is urgent, our expectations are high.

War stoppers!

Every screw stopper from beer or similar bottles contains rubber, even apart from its rubber ring. Millions of these stoppers are wasted every year and yet rubber is a vital necessity of war. Every stopper replaced in an empty bottle and returned promptly to the supplier saves the need for a new one.

What do I do...?

I make absolutely certain I put this

back in the bottle!

Issued by the Ministry of Information
Space presented to the Nation by the Brewers' Society

At a time when almost everything was in short supply, even bottle stoppers were recycled. (*Picture Post*)

In fact, the aluminium collected was never used to make a single Spitfire or Hurricane – it wasn't of sufficiently high grade.

But if contributing pots and pans wasn't exactly a war-winning gesture, saving and giving money definitely was. This led to Beaverbrook's next campaign, which he called 'The Spitfire Fund'. This priced, rather arbitrarily, a Spitfire at £5,000. Lord Beaverbrook even broke the money down into chunks: 6*d* paid for a rivet, an engine cost £1,750 and a bomb cost £20. Propaganda goes a long way in wartime.

CLOTHES RATIONING

In the history of the Second World War, Sunday, 1 June 1941 was an important day as far as Britain was concerned, not because there was a big battle fought on that day but because it was the day clothes rationing was announced. The reason for clothes rationing was simple – reducing the production of civilian clothes saved raw materials and freed workers and factories to produce more important things, like military uniforms, tanks and planes.

The rationing system was very strict and difficult to live with. Every civilian was issued with sixty-six coupons a year. A woman's winter coat cost eighteen coupons; an unlined mac cost nine (or eleven, if it was made of wool); a woman's dress cost eleven; blouses, jumpers and shoes cost five coupons each (although men's shoes were seven); a pair of stockings cost two coupons; vests and knickers were three coupons each and bras and suspender belts one apiece.

A survey at the end of the first year of clothes rationing found that the majority of people had run out of coupons completely. And things went from bad to worse after that. In 1943, the coupon allowance was slashed from sixty-six to only forty. Many canny people decided that the trick was to buy or make clothes that would somehow be suitable to wear in winter, spring, summer or autumn.

When full rationing was imposed, each adult in the country was only allowed one new outfit a year. To save material, the width of the lapels on men's jackets and the number of buttons was limited to three, with no buttons at all on cuffs, and trousers were now sold without turn-ups. (Many men were adamant they couldn't wear trousers without turn-ups, so deliberately bought trousers which were too long and then turned them up.) Trouser legs could be no wider than 19in (48cm) at the bottom. Similarly, men's socks, which had previously come up to their knees, were now limited to just 9in.

Women had it even worse. Out went frills and lace, the permitted width of the gusset in knickers was cut right down, skirts were made shorter and straighter, and pleats were almost a sin. And to make matters even worse, heels on shoes were to be no more than 2in (5cm) high. Different women reacted in different ways to clothes rationing. **Lorna Green** wrote:

> As I was a student, clothes rationing didn't worry me overmuch. Instead of stockings we wore knee-length socks. I made one winter skirt from a blanket and commandeered brown linen curtains from a friend to make a somewhat skimpy summer dress.

But soon after that, **Lorna** married a fellow medical student and for her wedding trousseau she made a huge effort:

> I had a new dress and coat as well as shoes, some undies and glorious flame-coloured pyjamas. My mother and her friends contributed coupons and the great-aunts sent some too, with reluctance. I couldn't think why they should worry about clothes at their age!

But back to **HJF**'s diaries. From here on, the various methods she employed to get round clothes rationing became almost an obsession. On 10 June 1941, a week after clothes rationing had first been introduced, she wrote, 'Bought 2oz. of wool with my first Clothing Coupons'. Other entries include:

> 26 August 1941: Bought Jean a black pinafore frock to wear with any colour jumper.

> 28 August: Bought Jean a pair of lace stockings at Brights at 4/11*d* a pair.

> 29 August: Visited furrier with regard to making my antelope coat fit Jean.

The following spring, she spent a lot of money and ingenuity on her daughter Jean, who was going away to teacher training college in Bedford:

> 6 March 1942: Bought 6 dozen initials with full name to sew on Jean's clothes and bed linen for Bedford College for 5/11*d*. Went to Baker's to buy

some of her outfit: mackintosh £2 15s 0d. At Brights 2 pairs of sheets with pillowcases to match, one pair corn colour and the other pale green. Also two serviettes making a total of £5 1s 2d.

Jean, by this time, wasn't really a child but for all mothers of growing children, buying clothes was a major problem which was only partly solved by an invention of the WVS: Clothing Exchanges. Mothers were encouraged to bring in clothes which their children had grown out of. Each item was then given a certain number of points by the WVS volunteer and clothes the next size up could be purchased with the points.

Alternatively, some mothers resorted to having clothes made for their children by local tailors or dressmakers, presumably because it saved money and helped to get round rationing. **Patricia Roffe**, from Rotherhithe in London, remembered:

My mother used to take me to a Jewish dressmaker's shop in Spitalfields to have clothes made for me. She was very good with money, my mother. When they said how much it would cost to make a dress or a coat for me, she always used to say, 'That's far too much. I'm not paying that!' and walk out. Then the dressmaker used to come after us and say, 'All right, all right, I'll make it for a bit less.' She drove a hard bargain, my mother, but I just remember how embarrassed I was.

On 4 May 1943, **HJF** made a reference to Utility Clothes for the first time, 'Bought Daddy two Utility Shirts with two collars at Hope's – 14 coupons.' In fact, Utility Clothes were introduced by the government at the end of 1941. They were on the way to being a civilian uniform – materials were ordered by the government and produced under strict government controls. Among other restrictions, the length of 'Daddy's' shirts was limited:

4 October 1944: Bought Daddy two pairs of pants and two pairs of socks which came to 10 points.

12 December: Bought two pairs of utility stockings, not fully fashioned, for 3/6d a pair. This is all I could obtain after visiting several drapers. Made a crocheted white string handbag for Jean with a long shoulder strap, Which is now all the fashion for young girls to carry.

And by this late stage of the war, it wasn't just clothes that were in short supply:

> 2 April 1945: Spring-cleaned my front sitting room and my curtains went to pieces in the water. I am dismayed as I shall have to give up many coupons to buy another pair. This means no suit or coat this year.

To have to make a choice between curtains or a coat illustrates just how tight rationing had become, by this time.

Towards the end of the war, the royal family took the opportunity to demonstrate that clothes rationing affected everyone – even royalty. They made it known that Princess Elizabeth, during the war, had always been a great collector of clothes coupons and eventually they came in very handy when she married Prince Philip in 1947. She wore a wedding dress made of material purchased using her saved up clothing coupons. (Prior to the wedding, she was also given hundreds more clothing coupons by women from all over the country to help make her dress. She, or rather court officials, dutifully returned the coupons as it was illegal for them to be given away in the first place.)

Knitting

Another aspect of clothes rationing was the national campaign to knit, whenever and wherever possible. The government's knitting scheme was set up at the start of the war, using slogans like 'England expects – knit your bit'. Many knitting patterns were given away free, while wool was sent to schools so that children could knit gloves, scarves and balaclavas. Wool was also supplied to Women's Institutes and they used it to make over 22 million knitted garments for the Red Cross – an astonishing sixty-seven garments per member. Parcels of their knitwear were sent to prisoners of war as well as to troops.

The government publicity machine never tired of sending photos to newspapers and magazines showing women of all ages and classes 'Knitting for Britain', at home, on trains and in factory canteens. And given the huge demand for wool, women were encouraged to go through their pre-war wardrobes, and their husbands', in search of old jumpers and sweaters so they could be painstakingly unravelled and the wool used again – and again. In addition, many women even combed the fur of their dogs and cats for 'wool' to spin into thread.

Rosemary Baker described how, as a young girl living in Nottinghamshire with her widowed mother, she was taught to knit at a very early age:

> I was about 6 when I first learnt – I never used a pattern or anything. I remember wool was in very short supply so it was my job to find all the old woollen jumpers which my father had worn, unravel them, wind the skeins of wool round the back of a chair and then wash the wool to get the wrinkles out. I lost count of the number of things I knitted during the war!

But knitting didn't have to be a solitary activity. Knitting circles among women became extremely popular and the Sidar Wool Company made a point of providing them with the specially dyed khaki, navy blue, air force blue and grey wool. This was then knitted into any number of caps and balaclavas, sweaters and pullovers, not to mention the ubiquitous socks and gloves.

HJF was also a capable knitter, although getting hold of the right wool was sometimes difficult:

> 7 October 1941: I tried to buy khaki coloured wool to make two pairs of gloves for A and R who are in the services but the shop would not serve it to me without a WVS voucher.

After that she continued to knit, although taking care not to break any rules. On 3 October 1944, she wrote:

> Nannie came to tea and brought me 4 oz. of pink baby wool to knit a coatee for a child in a liberated country, together with typewritten instructions as to measurements and stitch. She tells me that when made the garment will be weighed to see if the correct amount of wool given me has been used.

Make Do and Mend

To reinforce the message that everyone needed to make the most of what they'd got, the rather dull-sounding Board of Trade launched a campaign in 1943, which it dubbed 'Make Do and Mend'. Its remit was to 'help you to get the last possible ounce of wear out of all your clothes and household things' and its stated aim was 'not merely to revive the lost art of darning and patching, but to raise morale by showing how old clothes can be turned into really smart and attractive new ones'. For this purpose, the Board of Trade also organised over 5,000 classes in village halls and works canteens all over the country, teaching all and sundry how to darn, patch, sew and mend.

There was also an advertising campaign featuring Mrs Sew-and-Sew, who had endless wacky suggestions like making dressing gowns from worn-out bedspreads, sheets turned sides to middle, 'patriotic' patches on worn-out knees and elbows, men's jackets transformed into boys' or girls' coats, men's shirts into children's pyjamas and so on.

Vera Bartlett said this about making do and mending:

With two small children, I had to make do and mend a lot. I remember, for example, that I had an old Singer sewing machine, the sort where you have to turn a handle, and with it I made the children siren suits out of old army blankets. Sheets I had to top and tail, old towels were cut up to make face flannels and very old, worn-out sheets became handkerchiefs.

Even worn-out ties could be reused. (*Picture Post*)

Barbara Steadman told me one story of great ingenuity, and bravery, in the face of clothes rationing:

> My father was working as an ARP warden in Bristol and one of his jobs was to spot German parachute mines as they floated down under their parachutes. He then had to get to them in time and detach the land mine from the parachute which was made of pale-yellow silk. After that, he took the parachute to the local ARP headquarters and from there the material was made into beautiful underwear!

When it came to making do and mending, **HJF** had this to say:

> 11 November 1941: Cut tail off Daddy's shirt and made a new collar. Patched the tail with fine white sheeting. His tail is now around his neck!

> 9 March 1942: Commenced to make a blouse for Jean out of four old check dusters – these are couponless!

So her daughter Jean went off to college wearing a blouse made out of four old checked dusters.

> 7 April 1942: Bought two woollen car rugs to make coats for Jean and Daddy.

> 18 May 1943: I took a silk stocking to be repaired as they only charge 6*d* a ladder, whatever length it is. Cut out two overalls from blackout material which does not require clothing coupons and made the first one very successfully.

> 16 April 1942: As it was a lovely sunny afternoon, Jean and I lay in the courtyard on our camp beds and tried to brown our legs so as to be able to go without stockings in the warmer weather and thus save coupons for the winter.

A week later, she wrote, 'Made three toys from an old coat. A pony with a brown woollen mane and tail, a duck with yellow beak and a teddy bear. I stuffed them with clean old stockings.'

Eleanor Frost's mother was also a keen make do and mender. On 3 May 1944, she wrote, 'Mater called for some coloured wool to mend a jumper. I searched my needlework bag and found just the colour she wanted.'

As a postscript to these stories of clothes rationing and making do and mending, towards the end of the war the RAF decided that their airmen no longer needed what they called 'Escape and Evasion' maps of northern Italy. These were printed on silk to save weight and sewn into the airmen's flying suits, making them easy to hide in case they were shot down.

There was, as a result, a sudden and unexpected supply of fine silk in the shops, which was ideal material for making into women's underwear. The only problem was the silk had maps printed on both sides. In fact, an exhibit in the Imperial War Museum is what they describe as, 'A ladies bra and knickers set made from a silk map of Italy; the front of the bra shows the cities of Trieste and Milan whilst the knickers show northern and central Italy.'

9

Not All Doom and Gloom

The British people, and women in particular, may have needed distraction and light relief during the war but there was very little available. For a start, there was no television to watch – all BBC programmes were shut down in 1939 because it was feared the signals would in some way help German bombers. And, more to the point, there were fewer than 20,000 sets in the entire country.

Infinitely more popular was the radio, or 'wireless', as most people called it, although when it came to radio listening there wasn't much choice. There was only the Home Service, and to begin with, this was exceedingly monotonous – the news, followed by official announcements, followed by the almost inescapable Sandy Macpherson playing his theatre organ. In fact, in September 1939, Sandy MacPherson sometimes played for twelve hours a day, albeit with breaks. Some people became so bored they said they'd rather listen to German bombers overhead. The BBC responded by introducing more variety into its broadcasts, even including some comedy programmes.

As the war progressed, the *Nine O'Clock News* was a form of entertainment of sorts in most British homes. The British public developed a voracious appetite for news during the war, however bad it was. Water company records confirmed that most people delayed using the toilet or putting the kettle on until after the news had finished. One rather odd feature of the *Nine O'Clock News* is that the newsreaders, always men of course, had to wear full evening dress as they delivered their lines.

The news in the newspapers could also be regarded as a form of entertainment. Strict censorship, however, often made it a somewhat dull read because all newspapers were issued with 'Defence Notices', which prevented them from printing any hard news that would potentially be helpful to the

The radio, or wireless, was one of the few sources of entertainment during the war, hence this advertisement. (*Picture Post*)

enemy or, even worse, likely to sap morale. Details like how many people were killed, which parts of the city were bombed, the scale of destruction and so on, were impossible to find. Instead, Bristolians, in particular, had to be content with rousing but uninformative headlines like 'Nazi frightfulness came West last night'.

The news on the BBC was also censored, up to a point, and to make matters worse the BBC was banned from broadcasting the weather forecast – only references to the weather the previous day were permitted as forecasts might help the Luftwaffe plan their bombing operations. In spite of these restrictions and censorship the BBC managed to maintain a reputation for reasonably truthful reporting.

One odd aspect of the British insatiable appetite for war news and entertainment of sorts was the popularity of Lord Haw-Haw (see page 73). The government investigated why and found that 58 per cent of people interviewed said they listened because his version of the news was so fantastic that it was funny and 38 per cent because other people listened to him and talked to them about it.

Perhaps surprisingly, **HJF** admitted to listening to Lord Haw-Haw when she wrote on 16 October 1939, 'A German station is sneering on the air at our loss of the *Ark Royal*. It is horrible to listen to.' Perhaps even more surprising is **HJF**'s willingness to believe this piece of propaganda. In fact, the *Ark Royal* was not sunk until over a year later.

On 30 January 1940, **HJF** noted that she'd tuned in to Lord Haw-Haw again, 'Listened to Hitler on the wireless. He seems to have a terribly frightening voice, but that may be because I do not understand German.'

Janet Wayman was also a fan of Lord Haw-Haw:

Mum and I used to listen to him on the radio and when we heard the German bombers droning overhead she used to say, 'It's all right. They're not going to drop their bombs on us tonight. Lord Haw-Haw says they're off to wherever it was instead.' And she believed him.

Ivy Rogers also admitted that she and her family used to listen to Lord Haw-Haw. But according to her, they only listened because, 'He was so comical. We knew he was telling such lies.' Perhaps the British Government should be credited for not banning Lord Haw-Haw's German propaganda broadcasts, although this would have been almost impossible to enforce.

Needless to say, **Ivy Rogers** and her family also listened to the BBC, '*ITMA* was our favourite programme with Tommy Handley.' This was a popular radio show during the 1940s. *ITMA* was an acronym for '*It's That Man Again*' – a reference to Hitler and the frequency with which everyone referred to him. This half-hour programme was the high point of the week for many families. It was a character-based comedy show that made a point of satirising several prime wartime targets like rationing, queues, the blackout, shortages, bureaucracy and the black market. Some scenes were written less than an hour before being broadcast. It was so popular that if Hitler had chosen to invade England between 8.30 p.m. and 9 p.m. on a Thursday evening, he'd allegedly have met very little opposition because everyone would be glued to their radio sets.

Audrey Swindells had this to say about the programmes on the 'wireless':

The radio was also an important entertainment. We would listen to *ITMA* and other comedies and every Sunday afternoon we'd listen to J.B. Priestley, who would read a different short story that he had written each week. These stories were about peaceful times in rural villages and were most entertaining, interesting and relaxing.

Priestley's broadcast every Sunday had an audience of an estimated 16 million. Only Churchill was more popular with listeners. Later, however, Priestley's left-wing sympathies led to his talks being cancelled by the BBC.

Sticking with radio, with the arrival of the Americans came AFN – the American Forces Network – and this completely changed the listening habits of huge numbers of British people, women in particular. Out went Sandy MacPherson on his theatre organ and in came swing and jazz.

And the AFN didn't just broadcast music. It also had an up-to-the-minute news service and quickfire comedy shows with the likes of Bob Hope and Jack Benny. For GIs thousands of miles from home it was essential listening. For them, the BBC was far too slow, staid and stiff – too British, in other words. And it did what it set out to do: 'To Bring Yank Radio to Yanks in Britain and then in Europe.' But it was also hugely popular with British listeners.

Like **Ivy**, **Barbara Steadman** confirmed that the radio was really the only form of entertainment available to most families, although not every family could be sure of having their own radio set:

In our house we didn't have electricity, so my father, who was very good at making things and had made himself a crystal set, had to run that radio with an accumulator instead of a battery. And that accumulator had to be taken to a house not far away to be recharged.

Enid Beebee, living down in Redruth, Cornwall, had a similar story to tell:

We did have one luxury in our house – a radio. My father had always been interested in radios and he bought one of the very first in Redruth. He rigged up an aerial for it, which hung from a pole at the end of our garden to the roof of the house. There was only one problem – to listen to it you had to wear earphones.

That was probably why **Enid** added, 'I think in the war, our family and friends and other people were really where we got our entertainment.'

Ivy Rogers would probably have agreed with that. She said:

Us children also used to play bagatelle and cards together. We also had a dart board on the wall – my two brothers were good at darts. Our house was often full of our friends – the front door was always open and people just used to walk in.

Ivy didn't just listen to the radio at home:

In the Wills Tobacco Factory where I worked, us girls used to talk a lot and at the same time, we also listened to music on the radio – dance music mostly, with people like Harry Ray and Geraldo.

Ivy almost certainly listened to the BBC's *Music While You Work* programme. At the height of the war, over 8,000 factories broadcast the programme at full volume to over 4 million factory workers, most of them women. It was the radio programme that was supposed to put a song in the listeners' hearts and thereby increase production. One manager reported that when the programme was off the air for a week, production fell by as much as 20 per cent.

There may not have been a 'Top 20' during the war, but one of the biggest hits of the entire war, as far as songs were concerned, was originally

German. British troops fighting in the deserts of North Africa heard the song 'Lili Marleen', sung by Marlene Dietrich, 'borrowed' it, and translated it into English, as 'My Lily of the Lamplight'. Also extremely popular were songs sung by the so-called forces' sweetheart, Vera Lynn.

Concert parties were also put on in factory canteens by ENSA. These varied in quality. Some had genuinely talented performers, who included Gracie Fields, Vera Lynn, George Formby, Tony Hancock and members of the post-war *Goon Show*. But others only had second-raters, hence the alternative 'translation' of the ENSA acronym – 'Every Night Something Awful'.

The maximum wage paid to ENSA performers was £10 a week, however famous or popular you were. Altogether, ENSA gave 2.5 million live performances during the war, at the rate of 5,000 a week. No wonder some of those performances were second rate.

You didn't have to be a professional to perform at ENSA concerts. **Dorothy Kears** had always been interested in singing and dancing:

> During the day I worked in the Wills Cigarette Factory but in 1943, I started going out with a young man called Eric who was the trumpeter in a dance band and he got me a job with ENSA. I did a bit of tap dancing and I became the singer with the band.

Similarly, **Iris Gillard**, who'd had piano lessons from the age of 7, was invited to play in a small, three-piece dance band to entertain wounded American troops in Frenchay Hospital, just outside Bristol:

> A soldier used to come and pick us up in his jeep and take us out there. I wasn't paid for these performances. We were given ice cream instead. Vanilla ice cream it was. I'd never had it before!

Joyce Morris also remembered another very different form of entertainment to ENSA concerts:

> I always used to go to the pictures every Saturday morning, to the local bug house or flea pit, as we used to call it. I remember we used to love watching Laurel and Hardy and the Marx Brothers. Those were silent films and there used to be a lady playing the piano for sound effects.

Joyce went to the cinema on Saturday mornings. Adults usually went in the evening, after work, when people were prepared to queue, seemingly for hours, to see the latest picture. Most were big-budget, made-in-Hollywood American musicals, westerns and comedies – the perfect antidote to the grey, bomb-cratered world outside. *Gone with the Wind* and *The Wizard of Oz*, for example, both came out in 1939 and were massive hits with British audiences. The British film industry, in contrast, was reduced to making low-budget semi-propaganda films like *The Lion Has Wings*, *In Which We Serve* and *Target for Tonight*.

Audrey Stacey also went to the cinema once a week, but with her mother:

We always used to go on a Friday. There were always the adverts, then the B film and then the main film. My dad didn't come with us. He used to go to the Red Lion for a pint or two of beer with his friends, men of course.

Myrtle Way also enjoyed going to the pictures, although in her case it definitely wasn't once a week because:

We were a big family – I had three sisters and two brothers. My father was a docker and didn't earn very much so he could only afford to take one of us at a time to the pictures and I remember how we always used to argue over whose turn it was.

Lorna McNab also came from a family with very little money to spend:

But occasionally, Mother would say to me, 'Let's go to the cinema.' There were two within walking distance and if her purse was empty she'd look at the bookshelves, gather up a handful of Penguin paperbacks and go into a shop called Day's. She might get one and sixpence, enough for one-and-a-half tickets. Not enough for ice creams as well though.

Enid King also came from a poor family:

We didn't even have enough money to go to the pictures. But luckily I had a friend called Betty, who went every Saturday and she used to tell me all about the film when we met on Monday morning.

By contrast, **HJF** certainly had enough money to go to the cinema, and the theatre. On 28 October 1939 she wrote, 'To the Prince's Theatre to see the play *Runaway Love*. It was very funny and quite a tonic for these sad days.'

When it came to entertainments, **Dr Mary Jones** said:

> I went to one or two dances at the university union which was in the Victoria Rooms in those days. We danced the Lambeth Walk and the Military Two Step but I don't remember learning the jitterbug. That came later, with the arrival of the Americans.
>
> But I didn't really have much time for a social life, despite the fact that the ratio of boys to girls in our year was 6:1. For entertainment, I remember going to parties with other students and also to concerts at the Colston Hall where the BBC Symphony Orchestra played frequently.

This perhaps wasn't surprising – the orchestra was evacuated to Bristol from London for the duration of the war.

Elizabeth Longney described her principal source of entertainment. She'd met a young American soldier called Glyn Rooney (see page 200):

> Glyn and I went dancing together many times, especially on Sunday nights at the Victoria Rooms after I'd been helping out at the Red Cross. The American Army had their own dance band, which they brought over from their camp in Warminster. Anyway, Glyn taught me how to jitterbug, tossing me over his shoulder and then pulling me through between his legs.

Americans as a source of entertainment in the later years of the war was a recurring theme. They were simply good fun and **Elizabeth** made the most of it:

> At other times, I used to go dancing out at the American camp in the grounds of Tyntesfield [a big country house, now owned by the National Trust, 4 miles from Bristol]. Army trucks used to come and pick us up and take us there. I was never short of partners to dance with, partly because I was a good dancer and partly because I always dressed well. I was a good knitter and I used to make beautiful jumpers, one of them made of blue angora, I remember.

Elizabeth finally summed up her relationship with Americans during the war, 'I had the time of my life when the Americans were in Bristol but unfortunately it couldn't, and it didn't, last.'

Margaret Walton left school at 14 and got a job in a greengrocer's shop. She didn't enjoy it, but she did enjoy spending the money she earned and that was her principal source of entertainment:

> What did I spend my money on? Well, make-up mostly and lipstick, in particular. It cost me 9*d* a stick and it was made by a company called Louis Phillipe and I think it was called 'Raspberry Red'. My mum said I was too young to wear lipstick and threw it away, so I took care to only wear it when I was out. I also wore a perfume called 'California Poppy', I remember.
>
> Another thing I bought from the chemists was a bottle of brown liquid which I used to rub onto my legs to make it look as if I was wearing nylons. My mother hated me doing that because the brown dye used to come off on the sheets in my bed and she used to have to wash them as best she could. Some girls I knew even used to draw a pencil line down the back of their legs to make it look more realistic. I didn't go that far. I thought it was a bit common. Anyway, I thought I looked quite pretty. Other people thought so too and I once won a competition for the best legs.

Rose Jennings had a very different way of being entertained. She listened to the news on the radio, of course, and in particular, 'to the speeches of Churchill – the whole country stopped to listen to him. The way he delivered those speeches gave us all courage. They were wonderful.' Whole families used to huddle round their wireless sets listening to the Prime Minister growling out his high-flown words.

His speech to the Commons on 18 June 1940 gives a flavour of what his speeches were like:

> Hitler knows that he will have to break us in this island or lose the war. If we can stand up to him, all Europe will be free and the life of the world will move forward into broad, sunlit uplands; but if we fail then the whole world, including the United States, and all that we have known and cared for, will sink into the abyss of a new dark age ... Let us brace ourselves to our duty and so bear ourselves that if the British Commonwealth and Empire lasts for a thousand years men will say, 'This was their finest hour.'

In contrast, **Ruby Spragg** had very little time for entertainment. She used to work such long hours loading and unloading goods trains at Temple Meads station (see page 136) that she didn't really have much time for listening to the radio:

I started work at 7.30 a.m. and finished at 5 p.m., with an hour off for lunch. I also used to work on Saturday mornings. I was still only a young girl really and at the end of the day I was very tired. So I never used to go out in the evening. I didn't have the money or the energy. I certainly never went dancing. Boyfriends? No, never. I thought boys were silly!

At home, the only entertainment we had was an old wind-up record player which my father had bought off a doorstep salesman. It was my job to wind up that gramophone and we used to listen to the songs and sing along with them. We all used to enjoy that.

On 13 January 1941, **HJF** wrote about another form of entertainment, or at least self-improvement, '7.30. The wireless broadcast physical jerks by an Instructor who sings. In my siren suit, I did the exercises with him.' However, the next day she wrote, 'For the second morning I did "jerks" at 7.30 a.m. in time with the singing Instructor. Today I cannot sit down through stiffness!'

On 22 February 1941, **HJF** wrote about her other primary source of entertainment. 'No siren last night. To the Hippodrome with Daddy. Sirens went during the performance and then later the All Clear, which was greeted with cheers.' So by this stage of the Blitz on Bristol, people were becoming quite blasé about air-raid sirens. There was no question of the performance ending prematurely or of the audience leaving to take shelter.

Just occasionally, **HJF**'s frequent visits to the theatre and cinema were interrupted. On 8 September 1943, she wrote, 'We went to the Embassy and the news was flashed up on the screen that Italy had surrendered. There were immediate cheers and clapping and everyone rose and sang "God Save the King".'

HJF sometimes ventured out of Bristol to the seaside resort of Weston-super-Mare, where there were other forms of entertainment on offer:

18 August 1943: In the afternoon we sat in the Bathing Pool and watched the judging for the best bathing costume, the best figure and the bonniest

baby. We also watched a Punch and Judy show on the sands ... After dinner we walked on the new pier and Jean took Daddy on the 'dodgems' – twice.

So even when there was a war on, traditional seaside entertainments were still on offer.

To sum up, opportunities to go out and have fun during the war were limited. But young, single women took every opportunity available to enjoy themselves. **Barbara Brown**, for one, clearly had the time of her life during the war:

It's hard to believe now that I was doing all these wonderful things. I was like another person. It was all frightfully enjoyable really. It was wartime, but somehow we still found time to lead a young person's life – to the full. Yes, looking back on it, we really did have a lot of fun and I can honestly say that for me at least it was a case of 'Oh what a lovely war'. I just had such a wonderful time.

Ted and **Vera Bartlett** (right), on their wedding day, just before the beginning of the war.

10

Love and Marriage

Before the Second World War, girls and boys, young men and women were relatively segregated by social conventions and perhaps fear of pregnancy. Dating, or courting, as it was called then, was a far more sedate, slow-motion affair. But during the war, all this changed rapidly and radically. There was a complete revolution in the way boys and girls met, dated, had sex and married. The stories told by the women in this book mirror this change dramatically.

A letter written to *Woman* magazine in 1942, ending 'Name withheld', exemplified what was going on:

I am serving in the Forces and find I am going to have a baby. Two men could be responsible. But I don't know which. Both have offered to marry me, but I can't decide which. Would it be better to throw them both over and make a fresh start?

The reply from *Woman*'s agony aunt accurately reflected the prevailing mores:

Much better. You don't love either of them and whoever marries you will never feel sure of you. Get over this trouble, make up your mind to be morally stronger in future and marry when you find a man you can really love, moreover a man who will respect you before marriage.

Elsie Proctor described how she married in a hurry but very soon regretted it:

I got married soon after the war started. I was 20 and he was 26 and in the navy. But I didn't really love him and I don't think he loved me. I suppose we got married because that's what everybody seemed to be doing in those early days of the war. We just assumed that death was perhaps just around the corner, for either of us or both of us, so we might as well have some fun while we still could. We had a very simple wedding – over my lunch hour would you believe it – and our honeymoon was a weekend in a seedy, seaside boarding house in Blackpool. Then he got on the train to Liverpool, where he joined his ship and disappeared from my life. Even then, I think we both knew that it had all been a terrible mistake.

Soon after that I joined the WRNS. We wrote to each other, of course, frequently at first, but less and less often until we just lost touch. That was the way it was during the war for lots and lots of young couples. Here today, gone tomorrow.

So war made an enormous difference to the normal patterns of courtship and marriage. For a start, opportunities for girls to mix with the opposite sex were hugely increased. Some made the most of it, others initially held back. **Diana England** had this to say:

I didn't know how babies were born until I was 16 or perhaps even 17. I don't think I was really interested in boys – I had ponies and Labradors instead of boyfriends. And anyway, I don't think I was pretty – I had straight hair and I wore flannel shorts and Aertex shirts rather than pretty dresses.

But I remember one boy who was a friend of my brother's. His name was Kenneth and I thought he was frightfully good-looking and we went sailing together on his dinghy. I thought I loved him, but he never even kissed me!

But then the war came and things all started to change. A battalion of the Ox and Bucks Regiment had a large camp in one of our fields and I went out with a young officer in the regiment. His name was Tony Villiers and this time I really fell in love. He came to visit me and my pony – he loved horses – almost every day and when he didn't, I was desperately disappointed. He once took me out to afternoon tea in Reading. I remember I wanted him to kiss me so much. But he never did.

My mother dismissed it as puppy love, although I was 18 at the time. I remember, though, that my mother gave me this advice, 'You must look after your most treasured possession,' she told me. Anyway, soon after that Tony Villiers joined the Grenadier Guards and I never saw him again.

After Tony Villiers left, I went out with another young officer called Brian Coleman. He was 25, which I thought was frightfully old and in order to see him I had to climb out of my bedroom window!

I remember once I was sitting on his knee and he said to me, 'Don't ever change, will you, Diana.' Then I asked him, 'Do you think about me all the time?' and after a long pause, he said, 'No, not really.' Anyway, he was in the Royal West Kent Regiment and he left soon after that. I heard later that he was killed at Monte Casino.

Joan Fell, from Exmouth, in Devon, had a similar experience:

It was about this time that I started going out with the brother of a friend of mine. His name was Edward Bradford and he'd learnt to fly before the war. Then he went into the RAF and became a Hurricane pilot and was soon promoted to flying officer. He used to send me flowers every week and we wrote lots of letters to each other. I suppose we were in love and I thought that we were engaged, unofficially at least. But then he was killed in a flying accident.

Enid King, who worked for most of the war in the Land Army, also told me about a wartime romance:

I had one serious boyfriend at this time. His name was Joe McGrath and he was an American soldier from Mississippi. He was quite a bit older than me – he was 21 and I was only 17. Anyway, after three months he asked me to marry him. I was horrified! 'I can't marry you,' I said, 'I can't leave my mum and go all the way to America.' He stopped seeing me after that, although I don't think I was very upset.

Enid then described how she first met her English husband:

I'll never forget one evening when me and a friend of mine called Vera went to the King's Arms for a drink. At closing time, which was 10 o'clock, I came out and because it was so dark with the blackout I fell into the arms of a young man, who luckily just happened to be passing. Anyway, we got talking and agreed to meet the next evening. That was a bit risky because neither of us really knew what the other one looked like because everything was so dark outside the pub. All I knew was that he was tall. But to cut a long story short, I married that man and we've been happily married ever since.

Kathleen Gates also described how she met her husband during the war:

I met him when I was only 16. Then he went into the Merchant Navy and was a gunner on merchant ships that sailed up and down the west coast of Africa. We used to write to each other regularly. Some of the letters got through. Lots of them didn't. His letters to me were censored so I never really knew where he was.

Anyway, we got married in 1941 and had our first son, Roger, in 1942. My husband just had time to meet his baby son before he went away again for three whole years.

Mary Tyson also had a romance with a young serviceman but, in her case, it didn't end in marriage:

He was a young RAF officer. I was engaged to him – for about three weeks. We were having a candlelit dinner together and he produced this most wonderful emerald engagement ring. But then two days later he was posted to Malta. I sent the ring back to him, in an envelope in the post. I liked him but I never actually wanted to marry him. I just wanted to wear that beautiful ring for a few weeks, I suppose. Did he get the ring? I don't know, to tell you the truth. I never heard from him again.

Enid Beebee, in stark contrast, didn't have such a good time with boys during the war. She lived in Redruth, Cornwall, where there was a strong chapel tradition, which affected her life:

We had two American soldiers billeted in the house next door but my mother wouldn't let me even speak to them. She was very, very strict! She was a Methodist, who believed that it was a sin to listen to the radio or even sew on a Sunday. Perhaps because she'd been brought up in Plymouth where there were so many sailors around, I was frequently told by her that servicemen were never to be trusted!

Anyway, my sister, who was eighteen months younger than me, was always interested in boys and boys were interested in her and my mother found this terribly difficult to accept. One way round it was to tell our mother on Sunday that we were going to distribute the flowers from our chapel to sick and infirm people in Redruth. But this didn't take half as long as we said, which gave us the chance to meet the local boys and even some of the local airmen from RAF Portreath. I remember the young Polish pilots, in particular. They were charming.

In many cases, the war had the effect of speeding up and intensifying relationships. While up at Oxford reading mathematics, **Brenda Gimson** had met another student, Anthony Gillingham:

When the war started, Anthony volunteered for the Fleet Air Arm and because he was a mathematician, he became a navigator. His job was to sit behind the pilot of a Swordfish, a very slow biplane with a torpedo slung

Brenda Gillingham when she was a student at Oxford.

Brenda with her husband Anthony in his Fleet Air Arm uniform, just before they decided to get married.

beneath it, attacking German ships including the *Bismarck*. Anyway, we sensibly agreed not to get married for three years. But then, because his job was so dangerous, we changed our minds.

Anthony himself wrote later:

Brenda and I felt that in the circumstances it seemed highly unlikely that we would both be around in three years so we decided to get married straight away, on 27 July 1940. A friend lent me his MG for the wedding. We then had a very short honeymoon, a weekend in the South Downs and then I drove back to Ford air station on Monday just in time for 08.00 parade!

Soon after their brief honeymoon, Anthony was sent to Scotland to complete his training and join a ship, HMS *Victorious*, the latest aircraft carrier. The ship was to be in the Rosyth Dockyard for another three days and was then due to go to sea for trials. Anthony booked a room in a hotel for two nights and rang Brenda to tell her the good news. **Brenda** remembered:

We met at the station and from there he took me by taxi to the dockyard to show me his new ship with great pride. But to his horror, *Victorious* had just cast off and was already 15ft away from the dockside. There had been a change of plan and *Victorious* was putting to sea at once. So we hurriedly kissed goodbye before Anthony stood on the hook of a crane and got the crane driver to swing him aboard.

I then watched as *Victorious* disappeared out to sea before returning to a miserable, lonely night at the hotel. I was so upset, I think I spent the whole train journey going back to England in tears and trying not to let the other passengers in my compartment see.

For the next two years, I continued to work as a mathematician/statistician for the Admiralty in Bath. Anthony used to come to see me when he was on leave. But I was sharing a tiny cottage with another girl and it was difficult to get any privacy. Of course, I desperately wanted to be with my husband, but I was told I couldn't leave my job. Finally, I found a rule that said that certain couples separated by the war could be reunited. So I joined my husband in Arbroath in Scotland where he'd just been posted and we rented a bed-sitting room in a fisherman's cottage almost on the beach. The beds were a very strange shape, I remember, 5ft long by 5ft wide, so we had to both get into the habit of sleeping diagonally.

Joan Hancox describes in her diary her similar experiences as the newly married wife of husband, Phil, who was in the Royal Navy. The couple got engaged in Birkenhead in June 1940, when Joan was 20 and Phil only a year older. They had previously agreed not to get married until after the war. But, as in so many cases, they changed their minds and brought forward the wedding to 17 May 1941.

For the next five months, the navy sent Sub-Lieutenant Philip Hancox off on a series of training courses to Campbeltown in Scotland. then Portsmouth and Plymouth. The newly married couple spent as much time as possible together in hotel rooms and lodging houses. Finally, **Joan** wrote in her diary on 10 November 1941:

> Phil got his papers to say that he was posted to HMS *Nubian*, a Cossack class destroyer. The blow was that he had to join it on the East Indies station. We were terribly upset. It seemed so awfully far away. We had to pack up all of Philip's things supposing that he'll be away for two years!

Joan just before she became engaged to Philip Hancox.

Philip and **Joan Hancox** on their wedding day.

He was to sail from Liverpool on Monday, 17th November 1941. It was awful to know that we had just one short weekend before he set off to the other side of the world. How cruel it seemed … Poor Phil set off amidst rain and tears. Please God bring him safely home again. Each day I will miss him, long for him and love him always.

What follows are scattered entries from **Joan**'s diary while he was away:

The weeks after Phil sailed I was so lonely. But God willing, one fine day, we shall live together in our new house in peace and happiness.

Whilst he was away in the East Indies I wrote twice a week to Phil and he wrote lots to me from Bombay, where he now was for which I'll be forever grateful. Apart from his return they were the one thing I always longed for. It was always a good day when I got a letter from Phil and he wrote such good ones. God bless him.

I miss Phil so terribly and I'm so grateful for all his letters. He has just left India in the repaired *Nubian* and gone to Malta to be stationed there.

Phil writes lots and on March 16th I got a huge and glorious bunch of flowers cabled by Phil. He is so loving, so sweet and considerate. I hope I'll be a good wife to him.

I had a wedding anniversary cable from Phil and a wonderful bunch of flowers including red roses. How awfully sweet of him. I mean my marriage vows now more than I ever did: to love, honour and obey. God bless him always.

I was awfully worried to hear from Phil that he's been wounded in the right arm by a bomb splinter but he writes that he's OK.

Phil has now been away for 2 years in November. What a lifetime it seems. Had a letter from him at the beginning of November saying that he wouldn't be home till May 1944. But my misery finally came to an end on 26th November 1943 when I got a cable 'Probably be with you in mid-December'. I was so awfully thrilled I couldn't think straight nor keep from smiling so I started to get my things straight for a wonderful homecoming.

Finally, she wrote on 9 December 1943:

> I got a cable from Phil to say that he's arrived safely in the UK and hopes to be seeing me soon. This just about put me in seventh heaven! I felt quite crazy with anticipation of seeing him again.
>
> 14 December: Phil rang me from Newcastle. His voice sounded quite strange and we didn't know what to say! I felt quite dazed.
>
> 18 December: Got a telegram to meet the 3.15 train at Lime Street [Liverpool] on Sunday. I feel so awfully happy and can hardly bare [*sic*] such happiness.
>
> 19 December: A cold Sunday but the most wonderful. I don't know how I managed to exist all morning and definitely could not eat any lunch. Everything is ready to give Phil such a wonderful welcome even yet it does not seem real that I should be seeing him today.
>
> I went over to Lime Street in the Wolseley which was all polished up for the great occasion. The train was an hour late and I got more nervous all the time. But at last it arrived. Phil walked up to the car looking more wonderful than ever I can remember. I felt absolutely dumb and bursting with joy and happiness. After one quick kiss we drove home for the first time and we both walked into 'Gateside' [their new house] together and what could be more wonderful after waiting to do it for 26 long months.
>
> Phil looks well though thin and we're so awfully happy that there just aren't words to describe it.
>
> Phil brought loads of luggage and masses of lovely presents; stockings, sandals, underclothes, material, powder, lipsticks, creams. He's so sweet and generous who could help but love him. I am so devotedly in love with him and hope with all my heart that I will always make him happy.
>
> We wish that he need not go away again. We do hope that this is the end of foreign service for the rest of the war. He has had a wonderful experience but does not want to repeat it! So our wonderful dream of living together at 'Gateside' has at last come true.

And so to New Year's Eve. I wasn't feeling too good so we had a gentle evening and Phil showed me films including the glorious one of our wedding. Just being together to say goodbye to 1943 and to welcome 1944 makes the whole world seem wonderful. We love each other so very much. Our love means to us devotion, friendship, truth, trust and so much more as well and may it continue to do so for many happy years to come. God bless you darling, both thee and thine.

21 January 1944: Phil joined HMS *Vesper*, another destroyer, in Liverpool so while she was still in dock Phil managed to get quite a few nights at home. *Vesper* is on the Atlantic convoy work, out a month and in a week but as she was so old and didn't take the bad weather well they were in quite a lot. Phil had odd nights at home and a few odd days leave till mid April when they [HMS *Vesper*] went off down south, I suppose for the future invasion of France.

6 June: The Allies landed in Normandy at 06.00. Truly great news. God bless and keep Phil safe.

Phil has to get ready to sail to West Africa on HMS *Eland*. A bitter, bitter blow that my angel Phil should have to go overseas again – but better than the Far East. We both feel broken-hearted but there is nothing to do other than make the most of things and get on with his packing.

Phil finally went off on the midnight train on Sunday, 6 November. Poor, dearest Phil. I do so wish there was something I could do to help him. Both of us are heartbroken and deeply unhappy but whatever happens please God bring Phil safely home to me – however long he is away. I will always love him, heart, body and soul.

Phil did come home safely and they remained married for over fifty years.
    Quick, spur-of-the-moment weddings were almost the new norm at the beginning of the war. **Vera Bartlett** had this to say:

Several of our friends got married at this time, some on embarkation leave just before they went off to fight with the BEF in France. Perhaps they got married too quickly due to the pressure of war because a lot of those marriages didn't last.

Ivy Rogers also remembered deciding to get married in a hurry to Ron Garraway, who was a paratrooper:

> I was at home when I got a telegram from Ron saying he was coming home on embarkation leave just before being sent off to fight in Norway and he would be arriving at Stapleton Road station at such and such a time. It was quite late at night and I'd just washed my hair and it was still wet. I just had time to put it in rollers and put a scarf over my head. Anyway, we met at the station – it was just like that film *Brief Encounters* – and we started to walk home together. And as we were walking, Ron dropped into the conversation that if we got married we could claim two marriage allowances. So, of course, I agreed.

Dorothy Kears also spoke about a wartime romance and then how she first met her future husband:

> Like all teenagers, I was far more interested in having a good time, going to the pictures, as we used to call it, and going ice-skating and dancing and looking for boyfriends. I met one boy in Weston. His name was Ken and he was a radio operator in the navy. He had a car which even had a radio in it. I was very impressed by that and I tried very hard to be grown up when I was with him. Then he went away. I wrote to him but then I heard that his ship had been sunk and he was missing. I'll never forget Ken – he was absolutely adorable.
>
> Soon after that, my life changed completely. I went ice-skating and I was standing by the side of the rink when a young man suddenly stopped right in front of me and with his hands on the rail either side of me. I noticed straight away that he had almost perfect white teeth. We got talking and I soon found out that his name was Dennis and we started going out together.
>
> But soon after that, he was called up into the army and because he was a very good engineer he was given a job travelling round to all the tank regiments, repairing and then test-driving them. Not long after that, we got married, when I was 21 and he was 22. Looking back on it, we were like two little children – we were so young. But we were happily married for sixty-four years.

Iris Gillard also had a whirlwind romance and a quick wedding:

I got married in 1940. It wasn't a big wedding – my husband only had forty-eight hours' leave. He'd asked me to marry him in a church-yard – I don't know why he chose that place. He thought it would be romantic, I suppose. But he didn't give me a ring or anything – he didn't have any money. But he did have enough money for an MG sports car and a motorbike – a Douglas, it was. It was wonderful.

I couldn't wait to get married – we were in love. Anyway, I got pregnant soon after that. I know there was a war on but I really wanted to have a baby. That was the reason you got married. I still loved him forty years later when he died in 1983.

Iris Gillard, whose husband was away fighting for most of the war.

Margaret Walton also told me about the first love in her life:

I started going out with an American. His name was Bob and he was a military policeman from Kentucky. On 7 December 1944, we became engaged. Fortunately for him, he wasn't sent off to fight in France but back to the States and there he made all the plans for our wedding. He even bought a house for the two of us but deliberately left it unfurnished so that I could decide on the furniture and drapes and so on. Meanwhile, I went up to the American Embassy in London and got all my emigration papers in order and even booked my passage on the next boat to America.

But then I went into work one day and in the canteen a young man looked at my engagement ring and said, 'It's a pity that you're not going to marry him!' And then he asked about the emigration papers I had with me and he took them and tore them up. Anyway, that man became my husband and we were happily married for thirty-seven years.

Of course, I had to write to Bob in the States and tell him that I wanted to break off our engagement and he was terribly upset. His mother wrote to my mother and told her how much I'd hurt him. I often wonder what happened to him after that, whether he was happily married and had children like I did. I suppose I'll never know.

As a matter of interest just over 70,000 British women did make the decision to marry Americans. Officially named Operation War Bride, the popular press dubbed it Operation Diaper Run since so many of them were pregnant. And in many cases, they were not exactly welcomed with open arms in America. Small-town residents often accused the incoming British women of stealing their local boys. There are no official statistics for how many of these transatlantic marriages ended in failure but there were probably many.

Mary Meaking, however, tells how she met and married her Englishman:

I met my future husband in 1941. I was at a dance when this RAF boy came up to me and asked me to dance. I was quite a good dancer and he definitely wasn't up to my standard, but I liked him anyway.

We first met on Monday evening and on Wednesday we agreed to go to another dance and then he introduced me to his parents. It was all happening quite quickly because he was only home on leave for two weeks, and during that time we met almost every day. Young couples like us did do things in a hurry in those days because you never really knew whether you'd meet again and you had to take your chances while you had them.

In fact, he admitted to me later that he knew when we first met he wanted to marry me. But I was much more cautious and less keen. I didn't want to be tied down when I was so young. I was only 20 and I wanted to roam a bit!

It turned out that he'd been in the RAF since he was only 15 – he lied about his age – and was a rigger and fitter. Soon after that, he was sent to the desert in Egypt and eventually he became a pilot of Liberators, whose job it was to fly out over the sea looking for German submarines. So for the next three years, while he was serving in the RAF and based in Scotland, we just continued to write to each other. Even after the war was over, he continued to fly troops home from India and the Middle East, still in the same Liberator. I sometimes think he loved that plane almost as much as me.

Eventually, we did get married, in our local parish church. My mother arranged it all. A friend who lived on the other side of the road was a dressmaker and somehow managed to get enough material together to make my wedding dress and we had our honeymoon in Blackpool.

Keith and **Peggy Turner** on their wedding day. Sadly, Keith's officer's uniform did not arrive in time.

Peggy Turner remembered very well how she had met and married her husband, Keith Turner:

I'd originally met him when we were at school together, although he was three years older than me and a prefect. We were both in the school production of *The Mikado* – we were both in the chorus. In the spring and summer of 1939, before war was declared, we spent as much time as possible together.

Then, when I was just 19, Keith and I got engaged. My mother was 'a bit niggardly', in Keith's opinion, because her only comment was, 'Well, you can get engaged but I don't want any more young marriages!'

Soon after that, Keith decided to volunteer rather than wait to be conscripted. After the usual period of initial training as a private, he was offered a commission and so began, looking back on it now, the most extraordinary period of my life – the war years. [For an account of the early years of their marriage, see page 158.]

We didn't take my mother's advice – we got married soon after that, in December 1940. I didn't wear a white dress – you couldn't get the material in those days. And Keith was supposed to wear his new, very smart officer's uniform but it didn't come through in time and he was dressed in his old army battle dress, which was very far from smart.

In contrast, towards the end of what was, for her, a quite dramatic war, **Rosemary Strydom** was in Rome, of all places, but still in the ATS and unmarried:

In April 1945, I met a young South African soldier by the name of John Strydom. He'd come with his father, whose name was also John, to fight in the same regiment, the Umvoti Mounted Rifles, which was attached to the British Army, even though neither of them had ever ridden a horse in their lives. Unfortunately, John Strydom Senior was at some stage captured by the Germans and nothing more was ever heard of him. Apparently, he had been captured and shot by the retreating Germans.

John Junior was at most of the dances and parties I went to and our relationship became very quickly more and more close. So much so that when I received an order three months later that I was to be posted to Austria, we had to make a decision whether to go our separate ways or get married. We decided on the latter. It was a question of now or never.

But before I could get married, I had to obtain the permission of my mother because I was under 21. She had certain reservations about my marrying a South African, although it didn't occur to her to ask whether he was Black or white! Anyway, we got married in the English church in Rome on 16 August 1945.

I wore a long, white dress, the material for which I had 'borrowed' from some American friends. Many American soldiers were getting married at that time to Italian girls they'd met and the US Army had arranged for a supply of wedding dress material to be sent over from the States. My bridesmaid, a friend in the ATS, wore a beautiful green dress, although I can't remember her name!

Since my father was no longer alive, I was given away by my commanding officer, Colonel Thesinger. No members of my family came to the wedding – by this time, my brother had left Rome and was fighting further north. But a lot of friends were there, both from the ATS and John's regiment.

We had a big party after the wedding in a house that John had managed to 'requisition' for the occasion. I drank spumante – I had progressed a bit from the weak shandies that I used to drink as a 17-year-old in London. The American friends who came all seemed to drink Coca-Cola but always with something stronger in it.

The next day we set off on our honeymoon in an army jeep. We drove as far as Lake Como, having stopped in Florence on the way. Fortunately for us, the British Army had requisitioned a lovely old house by the shores of the lake for officers on leave. John had learned enough Italian for us to get by – he was always very good at languages. He could speak Zulu and Afrikaans as well as English. It was a gorgeous place. And there, for two weeks, we started our married life. Despite the fact we'd only known each other for four months and made the decision to get married under duress, we were happily married for the next sixty-nine years.

Elizabeth Longney's account of a wartime romance was perhaps the most affecting. She worked full-time as a telephone operator in the centre of Bristol throughout the war but still found the time and the energy to volunteer for another job after her shift finished:

To make the most of my free time, I volunteered to help at the American Red Cross Club in Berkeley Square. It wasn't difficult work, I just had to wear a white overall with a red volunteer badge on it and help in the canteen, picking up plates and so on. But instead of being paid, I was given a peanut butter sandwich, a doughnut and a Coca-Cola. That was my Sunday night supper for two-and-a-half years.

Anyway, after I'd eaten I used to play table tennis. I was a good player because I learnt to play against my brother, who was seven years older than me. The Americans queued up to play against me because I told them the first one to beat me could walk me home. Needless to say, I contrived to lose to the boy who I fancied the look of the most.

There was one boy in particular. He was tall, blue-eyed, blonde and very, very good-looking. I've still got a photograph of him to prove it. His name was Glyn.

I suppose I fell in love with Glyn. To me, at that age, speaking and looking like he did, it was like going out with a film star. It also helped that he had a lovely uniform with a smart collar and tie which made him look like an officer in my eyes, certainly compared to the soldiers in the British Army, whose uniform was very rough and ordinary by comparison. It also helped that he could sometimes get me things like sugar and candy from the PX store.

I had the time of my life when I was with Glyn. But unfortunately, it couldn't last — and it didn't. I remember very clearly one evening in early June 1944. Glyn and I had arranged to meet in the usual place, at the usual time. But for some unaccountable reason, he didn't come. I waited and waited, becoming more and more anxious and unhappy. Finally, with a sense of foreboding which I'll never forget, I went home.

I never saw Glyn again. The next day was 6 June, D-Day, and when I listened to the BBC News I immediately understood why Glyn had never come that evening.

I wrote to him, of course, many, many times, but I never got a reply. It's possible that he just wasn't very good at writing letters – he was probably only a poor white boy from the Deep South after all. It's also possible that he was killed on the beaches because military policemen had a terribly dangerous job directing the landings. I'll never know.

After she told me this, I asked **Elizabeth** if she wanted me to tell her what happened to Glyn Rooney. She thought for a long time and then replied, 'No, I don't think I do.' In fact, I found out from American military war records that Glyn had indeed been killed on Omaha Beach on D-Day.

American GIs socialising with British women at a military hospital in 1944. (Everett Collection Inc/Alamy Stock Photo)

11

'Overpaid, Oversexed and Over Here'

The arrival of Americans in Britain in 1942 was like a breath of very fresh transatlantic air. For many girls and women in this country, they represented a wonderful source of light relief, entertainment and plain fun.

The first American servicemen began to arrive in January to start setting up military bases, barely a month after the US had declared war on Germany on 11 December 1941. From then on, this country was a giant military staging post in preparation for the Allied invasion of German-occupied mainland Europe, although this wasn't to come for another two-and-a-half years. In fact, by May 1944 there were just over 1.6 million American servicemen in Britain and by the end of the war, approximately 3 million Americans had come to this country en route to the fighting in France and then Germany itself.

While they were here, most were determined to have a good time. They were, after all, quite likely to be killed in the next few months, one way or another. So every evening they came into town from their camps looking for fun and entertainment – and women. And a lot of those locals made them feel more than welcome, perhaps because Americans were generous, almost to a fault. Before long, talk of Americans being 'brash, flash and easy with their cash' abounded. This wasn't altogether surprising because they were, after all, five times better paid than the average British soldier.

To make them still more attractive, they brought with them exotic commodities like Lucky Strike and Camel cigarettes, Coca-Cola and Pepsi Cola, Wrigleys and Juicy Fruit chewing gum, Hershey Bars, ice cream, nylon stockings and unheard-of luxuries like deodorant and aftershave. They also came with exotica like left-hand-drive Jeeps, pinball machines, jukeboxes and the jitterbug. One way or another, they were far better off than the hard-done-by British soldier, to the extent that a British soldier was allowed a miserly three sheets of toilet paper a day while American GIs received twenty-two sheets!

But perhaps their biggest attraction was their American accent. At a time when Hollywood dominated this country's cinema screens, the accent seemed hugely glamorous. And for many English women, that was enough – the smooth uniforms, the good looks and their generosity were added bonuses. Small wonder that by the end of the war over 70,000 British women became GI brides and over 9,000 illegitimate war babies were born as a result of Anglo–American sexual liaisons.

These, however, often had sad consequences. One social historian described how if a British woman did become pregnant and went to the commanding officer of the baby's father, she was invariably turned away with a denial that anyone of that name existed. The GI concerned was then posted away.

In contrast, many Americans had a pretty low opinion of their British hosts. In retaliation for the description 'overpaid, oversexed and over here', many Americans concluded that Brits were 'underpaid, undersexed and under Eisenhower'.

Perhaps unsurprisingly, the rate of venereal disease among American servicemen shot up soon after they arrived in this country. And this was despite a concerted campaign by the US military, which included the following advice:

- Manhood comes from healthy sex organs.
- Disease may ruin the sex organs and deprive a man of his health and happiness.
- Guard against venereal disease by staying away from 'easy' women.
- If you do not have self-control then do not fail to take safety measures.

Then came one last memorable admonition:

- Don't forget – put it on before you put it in.

In another publication, American GIs were given this down-to-earth advice:

Stop and think before you sound off about lukewarm beer or cold boiled potatoes, or the way English cigarettes taste. If British civilians look dowdy and badly dressed it's not because they don't like good clothes or know how to wear them. All of their clothing is rationed.

This advice might have also included the fact that many of the young women they met in the evening had just come off working a twelve-hour shift in a factory. No wonder they weren't necessarily looking their best.

One woman in particular, **Joan Caldwell**, remembered the arrival of the first Americans vividly:

I was sitting in a café at the top of Park Street, Bristol drinking a cup of coffee – well, they called it coffee, although I don't think it came from a real coffee bean. Anyway, there I was thinking about nothing in particular when I heard this low, rumbling noise which seemed to be getting louder and louder.

Eventually, I was curious to know what it was, so I got up and went to the door of the café and looked right, down Park Street. And there, to my astonishment, coming up the hill was a long line of tanks. That, in itself, wasn't so unusual – I was used to seeing British military vehicles of all sorts on the streets of Bristol. But these tanks were altogether different – they were American tanks and riding on top of each of them were American soldiers. Now, I'd never ever seen a real American in my life, only on the cinema screen.

And as they got closer, I couldn't help but notice how different they looked to the average British soldier. For a start, they were smiling broadly, they had beautiful white teeth and their uniforms were smart and well-pressed – very different from the crumpled, baggy battledress of the British soldiers in the pubs I used to go to.

And in particular, the commander of the first tank in the convoy had a big cigar in his mouth and he was waving it at the crowds of people who were now filling the pavements. Now that American soldier didn't exactly throw chewing gum and stockings to us girls – that would have been too corny! But instead, I remember very clearly that he, or one of his crew, had painted on the side of his tank, in glorious technicolour, a very graphic picture of a washing line and on that washing line was an assortment of women's knickers, some of them decidedly frilly and skimpy by the standards of those days. That, in itself, was shocking enough – we weren't used to that sort of saucy 'art' being on such open display. What really shocked me was what was written underneath in large, capital letters: 'ONE YANK AND THEY'RE OFF!'

Dorothy Kears said of the Americans:

> To me, those American officers were straight out of Hollywood. They had wonderful, smooth uniforms, smart collars and ties and polished shoes. Several of them asked me out on dates and they used to give me presents all the time, perfume, stockings, soap, that sort of thing. Lots of local girls also thought they looked wonderful. Outside our pub, there were often girls just waiting around hoping to meet an American. My father used to go outside and tell them to go away. Some of them did, some of them didn't.

She also remembered the arrival of Black Americans very clearly:

> During my time off work I used to help in my parents' pub and that pub was the first one that Americans came to after they finished work or training, so we served a lot of Americans. And some of them were Black! I remember that was the very first time I'd seen a Black man. But I noticed one thing – the white GIs never had anything to do with the Black soldiers.

This reference to Black Americans arriving in Britain introduced the thorny and troublesome fact that the American military brought with them racial segregation. Back home, many US states were still enforcing what were known as Jim Crow laws. These involved the strict separation of races. By law, Black people were permitted to use only separate bus and train waiting rooms, seats on all forms of public transport were designated 'White' or 'Black' and restaurants, cemeteries, public schools, cinemas, public toilets, elevators, phone booths and drinking fountains were all strictly segregated. Dating between men and women of different races was very much frowned upon and interracial marriages were strictly illegal in many states.

So what was life like for Black American servicemen in Britain, subject as they were here to the same laws of segregation as they were back home? Significantly, Black GIs were not expected to fight in combat units on the front line and many white Americans believed that Black soldiers should not be allowed to even enter the military because, in combat, they would be 'unreliable'.

As a result, thousands of Black servicemen arrived early in Britain because they were needed to build the camps for the white GIs who came soon after. And they also stayed on longer in this country than the average white soldier because they didn't have to cross the Channel to fight. This meant they had far more time to mix with the locals or, as one soldier put it, 'We could crash their parties, drink their beer and flirt with their girls.'[2]

In fact they were welcomed, for the most part, by the British and particularly British women, who had in many cases never seen a Black person before, let alone socialised with one. This was because there were, in the 1940s, probably less than 7,000 Black people in the entire British Isles and almost all of them were in ports like London, Liverpool and Cardiff.

This interracial fraternisation didn't go down at all well in some quarters. A post-war analysis of mail home revealed that many white American GIs were appalled by the sight of English women being seen in public with Black American soldiers. One white American lieutenant wrote in a letter home:

> One thing I noticed here and which I don't like is the fact that the English don't draw any color line. The English must be pretty ignorant. I can't see how a white girl could associate with a negro.[3]

A high-up in the American military, General William G. Weaver probably expressed the thinking of most of his white contemporaries:

> God created different races of mankind because he meant it. Our Lord Jesus Christ preached the same tenet, the grounds for which were that such unions would make the blood of the offspring impure.[4]

Racial tensions in the US Army were exacerbated by the fact that Black soldiers experienced a very different treatment while they were here. Britain was, after all, a non-segregated society, where they were usually positively welcomed. So much so that when the US military authorities in the town of Bamber Bridge in Yorkshire demanded that the town's pubs impose a colour bar, many landlords responded by putting up signs that read, 'BLACK TROOPS ONLY'.

But it would be wrong to assume that all British women were welcoming and unprejudiced. One woman in particular, Mrs May, the wife of the Vicar

---

2   From an article written by Alan Rice, University of Central Lancashire, 1 February 2021, in *Black History Monthly*.
3   Alan Rice, 'Black troops were welcome in Britain, but Jim Crow wasn't: the race riot of one night in June 1943', *The Conversation*, 22 June 2018.
4   Sabine Lee, 'A Forgotten Legacy of the Second World War', *Contemporary European History*, Vol. 20, No. 2 (May 2011).

of Worle, near Bristol, called as many women as possible to a meeting in her village. There, she gave them this very firm advice or code of conduct:

1 – If a local woman keeps a shop and a coloured soldier enters, she must serve him but she must do it as quickly as possible and indicate that she does not want him to come there again.
2 – If she is in a cinema and notices a coloured soldier next to her, she should move to another seat immediately.
3 – If she is walking on the pavement and a coloured soldier is coming towards her, she should cross to the other pavement.
4 – If she is in a shop and a coloured soldier enters, she should leave as soon as she has made her purchase.
5 – White women, of course, must have no social relationship with coloured troops.
6 – On no account must coloured troops be invited to the homes of white women.

Some women in her audience chose to disregard her 'advice' and sent it instead to a national newspaper – the *Sunday Pictorial* – which printed it on 6 September 1942. The British public were, for the most part, appalled and several women in the village of Worle made a point of inviting Black troops into their homes for tea.

In Bristol, all Americans were initially made welcome, and one place where they met was the Red Cross in leafy Berkeley Square in Clifton. On this subject **Elizabeth Longney** had this to say:

To begin with, there were Black and white American soldiers at the club, although they didn't mix much and it was made clear to me by the white Americans that if I were to dance with a Black boy I'd be immediately ostracised by the whites.

I'll never forget one of the Americans I went out with. His name was Glyn Rooney, he was from Georgia and he was in the Military Police. [For a description of Elizabeth's relationship with Glyn, see page 200.] I remember once I was walking with him along Park Row when I noticed four Black soldiers coming towards us. I made to step slightly aside but Glyn wasn't having any of that. He just walked straight on and told me never, ever to 'move aside for any goddam n*****s'.

And it wasn't just in Bristol that there was visible racial segregation. **Hazel Bray** was a teacher in Buckfastleigh, south Devon, in 1944:

As D-Day approached there were more and more American soldiers around here. They were everywhere. One thing I remember clearly, there were two big US Army camps either side of the A38 near Chudleigh. Why two? Because one was for white American soldiers, the other for Black soldiers. I talked to both of them sometimes, although I admit I was a bit frightened of the Black soldiers at first. There weren't too many Black people in south Devon – there still aren't, in fact.

Ruby Spragg worked at Temple Meads station but occasionally still had the time and energy to go dancing after work:

When the Americans arrived, a lot of the girls I knew had a wonderful time. But I never went out with any of them. Of course, there were Black and white American soldiers. The English girls didn't use to mind who they danced with – they weren't usually colour prejudiced – but the white Americans got very angry if a girl danced with a Black man and there were often fights.

My sister Ivy used to dance with a lot of Americans, Black and white. She had a wonderful time during the war. And one of my friends got so friendly with an American that she ended up marrying him. I was invited to the wedding, I remember.

When it came to Black men dancing with English women, the jitterbug soon became the dance of choice for both of them. One Black American GI, Cleather Hathcock, had this to say:

At that time, the jitterbug was in and the Blacks would get a buggin' and the English just loved that. We would go into a dance hall and just take over the place because everybody wanted to learn how to do that American dance! They went wild over that.

In fact, dance halls were wonderful meeting places for young GIs and single British girls and, in many cases, young married women with their husbands away.

One of the women I spoke to told me about her auntie, but only on condition that I didn't include her full name:

> Her husband was a prisoner of war in Japan but when the Americans arrived in Bristol she made the most of it and had an affair with an American soldier – and he was Black! Our family disapproved, not surprisingly, but that didn't stop her.

HJF also mentioned the Americans many times in her diaries, particularly in connection with her daughter, Jean. On Sunday, 9 January 1944, she wrote:

> An American officer whom Jean met at a dance rang up this morning and asked for Jean, but she and her friend had gone to church. He eventually came round to tea and stayed talking until 10.30 p.m., leaving after a cup of coffee. He told us he was a Jew and a refugee from Germany but has now become a naturalised American. He told us that his mother and father were still in Germany.
>
> I am amazed that the American authorities send German Americans to fight against possibly their cousins and friends. Although he may be useful in the capacity of an interpreter, I am anxious in case the spirit of patriotism should return, or that if he were taken prisoner, information might be forced from him to save his parents. Still, I suppose the American Army know what they are doing and who am I to question?

After that, **HJF** continued to see various Americans around Bristol, although not always to talk to. On Friday, 4 February 1944 she wrote, 'Walked on the Downs taking Jockie. We watched American soldiers playing a team game but could not make anything out of it.'

The Americans and sport received another mention a few weeks later on 15 July: 'Watched cricket on the Clifton College playing field. Entrance fee 2/-. Several American soldiers were there but they said they could make nothing of it.'

HJF's contact with Americans was more personal when, on 2 April 1944, she wrote, 'Jean went to a dance at the Victoria Rooms and an American soldier asked to see her home.' The next day she wrote, 'The American soldier came to tea. He has been through a good deal whilst in Africa and has an old shrapnel wound in his leg.'

4 April: Jean went to another dance at the Victoria Rooms and another American saw her home.

8 April: Bob, the American sergeant, called at 1.30 p.m. and asked if he could take Jean to the zoo. They went and returned home to tea. He comes from Chicago and is a nice, fair-haired, clean-looking boy of 22.

But there was a problem when it came to welcoming American servicemen into British homes. There were many stories of young GIs being offered meals as a gesture of Anglo–American friendship, only for the American, unaware of the strictness of food rationing in Britain, to consume his hosts' entire food ration for the week. In response, a short Ministry of Information film was made entitled 'Welcome to Britain', during which Americans visiting a British home were encouraged to take with them two tins of peaches, a box of chocolates and a bottle of Bourbon.

12 April: Bob the American rang up and asked if he could call at 6.30. He came and very kindly gave us four tickets to the Philharmonic concert at the Colston Hall tomorrow.

15 April: Bob, the American sergeant, brought his friend Bill to tea. They were both two strapping young men and darkened the doorway on entering. Bob's friend is an art teacher in a high school in Chicago. They brought two more tickets for another concert. I am rather embarrassed at this kindliness for if I offer to pay they refuse to accept the money.

On 3 May, despite the fact that Jean had by this time gone back to college in Bedford, the Americans still 'rang up to ask if they could call this evening. Later they rang up to say they were sorry they could not come as the lorry was engaged and they could not get transport.' The need for domesticity among many Americans was very strong it seems even if it meant visiting a middle-aged English couple whose daughter was away. On 6 May, 'Bob and Bill called at 2 p.m. and stayed an hour having a glass of cider.'

HJF's last mention of Jean's American boyfriends was on 5 June, when she wrote, 'Rome taken. Received a farewell letter from Bob the American thanking me for my kindness. So I suppose they are on the move.' HJF supposed correctly, as it turned out. The next day, 6 June, was D-Day.

Rosemary Strydom was an ATS with the British Army in Rome in 1944. She told me about her contact with American soldiers:

The British Army weren't the only ones in Rome at that time. The Americans had also arrived just before us and they were everywhere, for the most part having a good time. I was invited to many dances organised by the Americans and I had dates with some of the young soldiers I danced with. But in many cases, they wanted more than I wanted to give them!

Rosemary, in fact, met her future husband soon after that (see page 198).
Meanwhile, back in London, when it came to meeting Americans at dances, **Patricia Roffe** had this to say:

I'll never forget my weekly trips to Covent Garden. But I didn't go to the opera or the ballet. They weren't my cup of tea. I went to the dances they held at the Royal Opera House instead. There were lots of American soldiers at these dances and often the dance band was American with soldiers in uniform playing the music. The American soldiers I met were terribly polite! I remember that when I got up to go to the Ladies, they stood up. And then when I came back they stood up again. I don't think many English boys would do that, certainly not the ones I knew!

Peggy Hart also remembered the Americans well. She was working as a nurse in Bristol:

I came into contact with the Americans who'd taken over Frenchay Hospital in May 1942. They were always very romantic — they gave flowers to the girls they dated, and then later chewing gum, and what they called 'candy' and nylon stockings, of course. English boys never did that.
I went out with one or two of them. There was one in particular I remember, Charles Von Braunberg. He went off to fight on D-Day. I never knew what happened to him.

Joan Watkins was also working as a nurse in Bristol when the Americans arrived:

There were quite a few of them billeted in houses in our road. But unlike some of the older girls I knew, I never really liked them. To me, they seemed so old, although many of them were not much more than 18. A friend of mine called Joy got a part-time job helping at a canteen for American soldiers. I went along to help her. But, unfortunately, I found that most of the American soldiers I spoke to were desperately homesick and only wanted to talk about their families back home.

I did meet an American officer once. He offered to give me a lift back to Southmead Hospital, where I was working – in his jeep. But I think I was far more interested in being seen riding in a jeep than in the American who drove it.

I was very young and innocent in those days. I did go to dances, but only ballroom dancing, you understand, not the jitterbug, which some of my friends liked. I hated the idea of being thrown around in the air. No, thank you very much! Or does that make me sound like a bit of a prig?

Jean Morris felt the same way as **Joan Watkins** when it came to the jitterbug:

I often used to go dancing. I was a good dancer, but I only did the ballroom dances, you understand, the waltz and the quickstep and so on. I never went in for the jitterbug although a lot of my friends did. No, I was never a 'jitterbugger', as we used to call them!

The jitterbug and the jive perhaps reflected how much pent-up energy young GIs had. They were literally fighting fit and they wanted everyone to know it. So instead of sedate waltzes and foxtrots, British dance halls now had athletic performances. In fact, the jitterbug was considered so wild that many British dance halls banned it for fear it would damage their sprung floors.

Kathleen Gates agreed with **Joan Watkins**. She wasn't so enamoured with the Americans either – which is probably just as well, since she was a married woman with her husband away in the RAF:

It wasn't all work while my husband was away. Occasionally I used to go dancing at the Victoria Rooms with friends. I only did ballroom dancing but there were lots of Americans there. I always found them a bit pushy, if you know what I mean. A lot of them were doing the jitterbug, throwing their partners up in the air and over their shoulders. That wasn't for me.

Lorna McNab was also very aware of the arrival of the Americans, although she was still relatively young at the time:

The Yanks walked around the streets of Clifton and thought our shops and pubs 'quaint'. I remember them as being tall, with long necks, slim-hipped with nice uniforms and forage caps on the side of their crewcuts. They wore brown boots or shoes, made of soft leather, not like the heavy black boots English soldiers had to wear. I saw General Eisenhower once, walking across Victoria Square. I didn't say anything to him.

The problem was I was only 13 at the time so I wasn't really girlfriend material. My parents sometimes invited two or three American officers to our home in the evening and I often came in from playing in Victoria Square to find them at the dining table, playing cards, eating sandwiches (Spam, a gift to my mother) and bottles of beer. They were always showing us pictures of their families back home in the US.

Lorna remembered another thing about the Americans:

A big tent with a raised dance floor was erected in The Glen at the top of Blackboy Hill. We used to crawl under the canvas flaps and gaze in wonder at them jitterbugging with local girls. It looked such fun and they were so glamorous! In my imagination, I went out on dates with them, but of course I was really too young.

Another girl who was just a bit too young to go out with any Americans was **Jean Grant**. She also described the arrival of Americans in Bristol with a degree of wishful thinking:

They were so handsome and generous. Some of the older girls I knew couldn't wait to flirt with them, and more. But I was too young, except that one day I remember I cycled all the way to Weston-super-Mare (about 20 miles) with a friend, left our bikes in a garage and then walked on the prom until we met with some American soldiers. We walked and talked with them I remember — but nothing more!

Margaret Walton's life was radically changed by the arrival of the Americans and she also had a different perspective on them:

They were billeted all over Bristol and there were American soldiers everywhere. It was all very exciting. Some of them were very young and inexperienced, and once, when we had an air raid and there were bombs falling, my mother found two young GIs cowering in our garden shed. She said to them, 'A fat lot of good you'll be if you have to go and fight.'

Elizabeth Longney, the woman who came into contact with Americans when working as a volunteer at the Red Cross Centre in Bristol, concluded her remarks about them by admitting:

After the Americans left it all went very quiet and a bit dull, by comparison. But while they were here, I can honestly say that, for me at least, I had the time of my life, mainly because I loved the Americans, I really did. And none of my family or close friends were killed and I just had such a wonderful, wonderful time when they were here.

12

Waiting and Hoping, and then the Day it all Ended

The Second World War involved many upheavals and very often the separation of families. Young men were sent off to fight, leaving their girlfriends and wives alone, often for years. And young women were compelled to leave home when they were conscripted into one of the armed services or required to take jobs and work away from home. For many of them, the war was a long period of waiting and hoping.

Mass conscription and the forced separation of families began as soon as war was declared. By the end of 1939, more than 1.5 million men had joined one of the armed services and by the end of the war that number had ballooned to 2.5 million. This obviously changed the lives of the men concerned but also changed the lives of their parents, wives and girlfriends.

HJF often referred to the effects of conscription in her diaries. Two weeks after war started, on 21 September 1939, she wrote, 'Greg, a family friend, called this evening in RAF uniform. It was a great shock to me, especially when I think of his wife and two sweet little girlies. How near home the war is creeping!'

On 25 February 1940, **HJF** wrote about a woman she met:

The woman's only son had just gone into the army, and she was crying. I tried to cheer her up. She told me that she had written to the King telling him that she had lost her husband in the 1914–18 War and now her only child had been called up to fight in this war, but she had received a reply from some Army department saying that nothing could be done. I expect there are many cases like hers, poor dear!

Enid Beebee, a young Cornish woman, described how she was separated from her husband for much of the war:

> Just before my 21st birthday, I started going out with a boy who went to the same church as us. Then, in 1942, we got married just before he was sent away to fight with the 1st Army in Egypt and then to Monte Cassino in Italy and after that to Crete where he took the German surrender. He was away for three long years and I missed him dreadfully. When he eventually came back, he was a different man. And I suppose I was a different woman.

Mary Thorpe had this similar story to tell about the homecoming of her husband:

> At last, he came home from the war and we were reunited as a family. While he was away, the children, when they were old enough, used to kiss their father's photograph before they went to bed. But his homecoming wasn't easy … He was a sergeant major and was used to instant obedience. He definitely wasn't used to living with small children and I felt very strongly that they were my children, not his, and resented it when he told them off. Their characters were already formed and he was a comparative stranger in their lives, and mine. I think looking back on it now, he was quite jealous of the attention I gave them. He felt, like me, that they were my children much more than his. But we got over it.

Peggy Hart also got married young, when she was just 18, in fact, and soon after that became pregnant. Her husband was sent to fight in France and Belgium and then in Greece:

> I didn't use to hear from him for weeks at a time. I didn't know where he was or what he was doing. I worried, of course I worried desperately, but that's how it was in the war. We were all in the same boat. But he eventually came back alive and I just felt so sorry for my friends who lost their boyfriends and husbands. I was just very lucky, I suppose.

Kathleen Gates also described the pain of separation:

> My husband just had time to meet his baby son before he went away for two whole years. I knew he had to go. I didn't complain. There were thousands

of young wives like me. I just had to accept it. I said goodbye to him at the station although I had no idea where he was going or if he was ever going to come back.

He did at last come home. But he hadn't seen his son for nearly three years and there was a distance between them which he had to overcome. It wasn't easy.

Rose Jennings wasn't separated from her boyfriend or husband but from her brothers, which she found almost as hard:

One of my two brothers went into the RAF. He was with the Intelligence Corps in the Middle East and then in Italy. I worried a lot about him because I don't think he was necessarily very brave or likely to be good at fighting. My other brother was in the army, fighting in the jungles of Burma. I worried about him, too, because he suffered badly from hay fever and I imagined that if he sneezed while Japanese soldiers were near he would give away their position. But he didn't sneeze, or at least he managed to survive the war. In fact, he came back almost cured of his hay fever.

I suppose my mother also worried about her sons during the war. She herself had lost a brother in the Great War, as she used to call it. But she was never very demonstrative, my mother, and she never expressed this anxiety or fear.

Diana England's much-loved brother Tony wasn't so lucky and Diana described her last meeting with him:

When Tony was on embarkation leave – he was being sent away to fight in North Africa – I was given compassionate leave so I could say goodbye to him. Just before he left he said, 'If anything happens to me, you can have my car.' It was his Baby Austin and it was his pride and joy. So after he went missing, presumed dead [see page 219], I took over his car and I loved it dearly and I kept it for years after the war, even after I'd got married. Eventually, my father-in-law insisted I get rid of it, so I sold it for £10. I remember I was very sad. It was one of my last links with my brother Tony.

Peggy Turner spent most of the war following her husband Keith from one posting to another. But to begin with, at least, they were separated:

I'll never forget the first time Keith left to go off and be a soldier. We drove to Temple Meads station in Bristol – his train was due to leave at 1 p.m. When the guard blew his whistle, I remember I said to him, 'I don't want to watch you go, darling' and then I just walked away, through the ticket barrier without looking back once. As soon as I was out of the station, I drove up to the Downs to be on my own and spent the whole afternoon in the car, just knitting him a balaclava and crying.

For the next few years, **Peggy** was relatively lucky. She wasn't separated from her husband Keith – she just had to put up with following him across the country. But in 1944 their luck, if that's what it was, ran out:

As fate and the demands of war would have it, Keith very soon after that was issued with tropical kit and ordered to embark on the long and danger-ous journey to Burma to fight the Japanese. Incredibly, I wasn't to see him again for two-and-a-half years. I was just left wondering whether I'd ever see him again, dreading the arrival of a telegram to say that he'd been taken prisoner or worse – killed.

Describing his departure for Burma, Keith himself wrote:

Mummy, Daddy and baby Lois spent the best part of the day together. At around 5 o'clock, we had a cup of tea and then I went to catch the last bus to the depot. When I went back into the room Pegs had the babe on her lap starting preparations for the night. Her face was low down over the child. I said simply, 'Bye bye baby Lois' and kissed her. Then I kissed Peg on the cheek, turned and left the room. Later I dared not think of the scene in that room I had just left. We have both confessed we never expected to see each other again.

Peggy then took up the story:

The whole time Keith was away I took my marriage vows very seriously and wrote to him regularly. It turned out those letters often arrived, not one by one as I had written them, but in big bundles which must have taken him hours to read. His letters to me were the same, very irregular and often many at the same time.

Finally came the end of war – VJ Day – the end of war with Japan. But I still had to hope that 9,000 miles away, my man had somehow survived. In fact, Keith and his regiment had to stay in Burma until 1947! They were mopping up resistance from Japanese soldiers who were still fighting, either because they hadn't heard of the Japanese surrender or because they refused to accept it.

I personally wrote to Stafford Cripps, a government minister, pointing out that Keith and his men had done more than their fair share of fighting and should be sent home immediately. The letter didn't seem to do much good. Finally, nearly two years after the end of the war in Europe, Keith returned to England and me and his family.

Keith described the family reunion:

We finally arrived in Southampton and were told that we would be disembarking the next day. However, during the afternoon, I noticed a phone kiosk on the quayside and some people appeared to be nipping off to make a call. At about six in the evening, I saw the kiosk was empty so I nipped in with a reverse charge call to Lydney where I came from. My brother answered. He was disposed to chat but I was curt. There was only one voice I wanted to hear and I was able to talk to the girl I'd dreamed of for nearly eighteen months.

The next day the Turner family were at last reunited. Keith again described what happened:

I reached Bristol Temple Meads at about 5.30 p.m. and there she was, as lovely as ever, the girl who had always been in my mind throughout everything. I could see my father pointing and I could hear her saying, 'There's Daddy, there's Daddy.' Pegs, bless her, had kept my memory green by showing Sue my photograph every day.

Walking to my home, my daughter took charge, chattering away and singing, obviously very happy. A quick cup of tea with my folks and then the last stage, to Lydney. As I walked through the door, a scrap who I had last seen as a bundle came tottering towards me. Pegs gasped, 'She can walk!' Grandma had been working hard in Peg's absence. I picked up Lois, hugged and kissed her – I was home!

Vera Bartlett also had a traumatic and very troubled war, separated for most of the time from her husband, Ted:

> At the beginning of the war, Ted had to spend all his time with his regiment and I could only see him in the evening when he was off-duty. We used to meet under a lamp-post and talk through the railings that surrounded the drill hall. And we were married!
>
> Then, in 1940, Ted was sent away to France to fight with the BEF. It was very difficult for me, particularly because I was pregnant. His leaving was postponed a couple of times, so I said goodbye to him three times altogether. He was sent to try to help the French Army resist the German invasion.
>
> Looking back on it now, if I'd known how desperate the fighting was round Dunkirk, I'd have worried much more. In fact, I didn't hear anything for ten whole days. The worst part of it was not knowing whether he was dead or alive.
>
> I remember going to the Post Office one day with a letter telling him that our first baby was born. I told them he was with the British Expeditionary Force in France and the name of his regiment but they said that it was no good because with all the fighting he was probably moving about the whole time so there was no way of contacting him. That really, really upset me.
>
> Anyway, I stayed in the nursing home for ten days after our first baby was born on 9 June, five days after the last troops had been evacuated from Dunkirk. But I still hadn't heard from Ted! I feared the worst, especially when the girl in the bed next to me was visited by her husband and he'd been evacuated from the beaches at Dunkirk. But then, just as I was beginning to give up hope, I finally heard news. I felt such tremendous relief when, at last, I got a message saying that my husband was still alive!
>
> It turned out that he was one of the very last to be evacuated from France, from Saint Valery-en-Caux, a considerable distance down the coast from Dunkirk. He told me later that he slid down a cliff onto the beach accompanied by a cow and got onto a waiting fishing boat. When safely on board, he and some friends opened a few bottles of wine that they'd managed to bring with them and then slept until they landed back in England. They'd been on the run for over a week and were totally exhausted.
>
> You'd think the British Army could surely have contacted me and told me of his escape. But no such luck. He was taken to London on a troop train and then sent on another train straight up to Newcastle, of all places,

and he only just had time to give someone on the station platform a telephone number on the back of a cigarette packet. It was the number of the bank where my father worked. That person phoned the bank to say simply that Ted was alive and OK.

Eventually he was given leave and at last he came to see me and the baby. He arrived at 6 o'clock in the morning, took one look in the cot, and said simply, 'Is that it?' It seems he just couldn't wait to get down to the drill hall because he was desperate to find out how many of his friends had got back safely. His brother, he found out, had been wounded and taken prisoner but many of his friends were killed. Some of them were boys I remember dancing with.

From then on, I was more or less on my own with the children for the rest of the war. It wasn't easy. After he came back from Dunkirk, Ted worked for a short time as a guard at a prisoner-of-war camp in Surrey. Fortunately, he was with me on leave when our second child, our daughter Tina, was born in 1942. He helped me to look after Teddy and the new baby. But as soon as his leave ended, I developed milk fever and was seriously ill. This was very hard with two babies to look after! And soon after that, he was sent away again, this time to fight in North Africa. By that time, I discovered I was three months pregnant with our third child.

From there, Ted was sent to fight in Sicily and then mainland Italy – including the Battle of Monte Casino. He was away for two-and-a-half years altogether, leaving me on my own with three very young children. But a lot of young mothers were in the same boat as me so I couldn't complain.

Of course, I never went out in the evening, I never had a drink, I had no social life at all because it was impossible to get a babysitter – everybody was too busy doing war work or working as an air-raid warden. The only time I left that pokey flat was when I went shopping. Then, when I got home, I had to climb three flights of stairs with all the shopping and three babies and all their paraphernalia. Sometimes I used to come back with nothing at all because nothing was available. That was quite serious, because I had almost nothing to fall back on.

All in all, I think it was easier for the troops like Ted because at least they were always together, while young mothers like me back home were usually on our own and whatever happened, we had to deal with it. I couldn't just phone for help, even if I'd had a telephone. I had to learn to change plugs, deal with leaks, mend broken windows all on my own – mostly from magazines. And sometimes I had to help other people as well.

I remember once I was woken by the man in the upstairs flat to say that water was pouring in from his ceiling because damage from flying shrapnel had blown half his roof away during an air raid. So I had to leave my children and spend the rest of the night finding buckets and saucepans and mopping up generally.

Another time I was in my flat with three small children when there was a loud knocking on my door. It was another man, who'd come to tell me that the chimney in the house was on fire. It certainly wasn't from my fire – I couldn't afford the coal – so we both went up to the flat above and hammered on the door but nobody answered – the woman who lived there was out at work as an ARP warden. So anyway, we got in and the whole flat was full of dense smoke and we couldn't see a thing. But between us we managed to put the fire out before the whole house went up in flames. The funny thing was, I don't think the woman who lived in that flat ever came and thanked me. She just complained when one of my babies cried.

At the end of my last interview with **Vera**, she became almost philosophical when she summed up her experiences during the war:

> Looking back on it, I suppose I was foolhardy to have three children in wartime but I wanted them and I was a good mother and they were never hungry or frightened. In fact, the only time Teddy, the oldest, ever screamed was when he lost his pyjama trousers as I was running downstairs in an air raid with a child under each arm.

Vera died at the age of 101. In her funeral notice, it said simply, 'Vera requested that her funeral should be a celebration of a wonderful life and that only bright colours should be worn.' That was typical of **Vera** and the huge numbers of women who spent a lot of the war on their own, separated by war, desperately waiting for news and finally being reunited.

D-Day

What almost all these women were waiting for was, of course, D-Day, then VE Day and finally VJ Day.

The build-up to D-Day was long and protracted. It started in January 1942, when the first American forces arrived in this country and continued for the next two-and-a-half years. It took this long because it was the largest seaborne invasion in history – by far. The operation marked the beginning of the liberation of German-occupied France and subsequently of Western Europe. (D incidentally is short for 'Day' and the tautological name was given to what had, up until then, been code-named Operation Overlord.)

Just before midnight on 5 June 1944, Churchill asked his wife Clemmie whether she had any idea that by the time she woke up it was possible that 20,000 men could be dead. General Eisenhower, meanwhile, in overall charge of the operation, had just finished his fourth packet of Camels – his way of coping with the stress.

On the night of 5/6 June 1944, amphibious landings were preceded by a massive aerial and naval bombardment. This was followed by the landing of 24,000 airborne troops shortly after midnight. The invasion fleet comprised 6,939 vessels: 1,213 warships, 4,126 landing craft of various types, 736 ancillary craft and 864 merchant ships.

Allied infantry and armoured divisions began landing on the coast of France at 6.30 a.m. A 50-mile stretch of the Normandy coastline was divided into five sectors: Utah, Omaha, Gold, Juno and Sword. The British landed at Sword and Gold beaches, the Canadians at Juno beach and the Americans at Utah and Omaha.

Allied casualties on the first day were 4,414, not the 20,000 that Churchill had pessimistically predicted. The Germans lost 1,000 men. French civilian casualties were estimated at 3,000.

At 9.32 a.m. on 6 June 1944, the BBC broadcaster John Snagge made the following announcement: 'D-Day has come …The long-expected second front has at last opened.'

Several women told me about how they experienced the build-up to D-Day and then the day itself. **Suzanne Best** said:

As D-Day got nearer and nearer, the whole of Hampshire seemed to be taken over by Canadian and American troops, guns and tanks. In fact, the whole of the south coast near where we lived was out of bounds.

I remember the weather was particularly hot at the beginning of that June and the roads and lanes round our school were ripped up as the tarmac melted and then heavy tanks and armoured personnel carriers drove along them.

And I also remember some of the 'boys' who were going to take part in the imminent invasion. They were Canadians who had a camp under canvas in the woods near our boarding school. Unfortunately, the young soldiers were strictly out of bounds to us girls, even when they took over our playing fields to play baseball. All of them were just hanging around, waiting to go. Some of them looked so young, only about our age. We waved to them from a distance and smiled, and one girl even blew them kisses, but that was the closest we ever got.

It's sad really, those boys must have known full well where they were going in the near future and what they had to do when they got there. And secretly, they must have been very scared, knowing perhaps they were soon going to die or be badly injured.

Looking back on it now, I remember there was an almost palpable feeling of expectation in the air. Everyone knew why they were there. What we didn't know was which beaches in France they were going to land on and, more to the point, when. But then, suddenly, they were all gone. And Hampshire returned more or less to normal.

In Bristol, preparations for the expected exodus were also well advanced. One young mother remembered on a warm day pushing her pram past some houses which all had their windows wide open and on the window sills were sitting a number of American GIs. They waved at her and then some of them proceeded to literally throw English coins at her, or rather, in her direction.

The young woman was amazed by their generosity until, a few days later, she understood the reason for it: D-Day. They knew they were going to be leaving England very soon and would have no use at all for their English money after that.

Audrey Swindells also remembered the build-up to D-Day very clearly. She was 16 and living with her parents just outside Felixstowe, on the east coast. She wrote:

The whole area was bursting with military personnel. Daddy had an old friend called Gordon who he used to play chess with. He was in the navy and Daddy was surprised one day when Gordon arrived unexpectedly with a briefcase containing many of his personal details. He asked if Daddy would keep it in his safe. He also told us that he would be unable to see us for a while, as all naval personnel were to be locked in their base.

'Something's up!' Daddy said, and I soon knew that to be true because armoured vehicles started to drive by full of troops. They were so close and continuous that it was impossible to cross the road. This mass migration of military vehicles continued day and night for two or three days. It then suddenly ceased.

Audrey then added another interesting detail to her description of the build-up to D-Day:

> I was walking to the local shop to get something when a huge, black chauf-feur-driven car appeared and I could see a lit cigar protruding from the back window. I felt sure it was Winston Churchill. Then when Gordon was free to see us again he told me that Churchill had indeed been to view the masses of camouflaged vehicles that were hidden along the banks of the Orwell and Stour Rivers because the operation had been delayed for a day due to poor weather.
>
> On the morning of 6 June 1944, Daddy returned from night duty and unusually he woke my mother rather earlier than she normally liked, but with a cuppa. He was talking loudly and excitedly so I went into their bed-room to hear him saying, 'We're not normally woken in the night, but I was up all night passing on coded signals. Then, when I came off-duty, I went to the top of the cliff and was amazed — as far as the eye could see, right across the bay, were amphibious boats and beside them enormous transport ships carrying armoured vehicles and tanks.' He then paused for a moment before adding, 'This is it — it's begun!'
>
> It was the morning of D-Day.

Meanwhile, **Enid Beebee** in Cornwall remembered this small detail of the build-up to D-Day, 'As D-Day approached, I remember a local disused railway cutting was completely netted over and used for storing huge num-bers of guns, lorries and tanks prior to the Normandy landings.' In fact, at that time, almost all roads leading towards the south coast of England were clogged with huge low-loaders carrying tanks and artillery, lorries and guns of all shapes and sizes and lorry-loads of troops kitted out and ready to fight.

Strangely, **HJF** hardly bothered to mention D-Day in her diary:

> 5 June: Rome taken. Strawberries today 2/6d a lb.

> 6 June: Our troops have landed on the continent. They are said to be air-borne and descending by parachute.

And that's it. In fact, it wasn't until four days later that she mentioned D-Day again:

> 11 June: Went to the Odeon to see the film of our men landing on the French beaches. Tuesday last is now called D-Day. The Mulberry Harbour was a wonderful asset to our landing craft. I admire the men who made it and kept the secret.

After that **HJF**'s references to the progress of the Allied armies through northern France were only intermittent. Typically, on 24 September she wrote, 'The wireless says our army has reached the airborne troops at Arnhem. I am so glad. Sent Jean the coat hangers and talcum powder she has asked for.'

Ruby Spragg, who worked for most of the war loading and unloading railway wagons, remembered D-Day, although a bit like **HJF**, she was underwhelmed:

> For a week before that day, 6 June 1944, I was doing shift work down at Temple Meads and I was on the later shift, starting at 10 o'clock, so I was having a lie-in. But at 7 o'clock my mother came into my bedroom when I was still fast asleep with a cup of tea for me. 'I've just heard the news,' she said, 'they've landed!'
> 'Who have?' I said.
> 'Our boys,' she said, 'in France.'
> 'Oh good,' I said, 'that'll do it.'
> 'God help our boys,' my mother kept saying. I think she was remembering the First World War and she was afraid it would end up like that – trench warfare again. And then I went back to sleep!

Brenda Gimson also remembered D-Day but for her, it was far more dramatic:

> I was in Surrey at the time. We looked up and saw hundreds of transport planes flying overhead towards France, escorted by fighters and towing transport gliders. The invasion of Europe had begun – at last!

Ivy Rogers, a cook in the WRNS, was stationed in a large hotel on the quayside in Southampton, temporarily commandeered by the navy and renamed HMS *Shrapnel*. The hotel functioned as the Centre of Combined

Operations leading up to D-Day and top-level meetings between Churchill and Eisenhower were held there:

> On 5 June, HMS *Shrapnel* was absolutely full of sailors, soldiers and marines, and out of the window I could see thousands and thousands of troops disembarking from train after train. Everyone knew something important was about to happen but they could only guess what it was and they weren't allowed to talk about it; 'Careless talk costs lives' and all that.
>
> Anyway, the next day I knew. The whole hotel was empty apart from us WRNS and on the station there were no troops to be seen. They'd all gone to take part in the D-Day landings and had left behind them what I can only describe as a ghost town. It felt really eerie.
>
> None of the officers I'd been cooking for came back and I never knew how many were killed on that first day, or after that. One of the girls I shared a room with was going out with an officer in the Marines. She never saw him again after D-Day.

This was a story that many women told me, with variations. Everyone was desperately busy, full of expectation, trepidation and, in some cases, real fear. And then, suddenly, as if the plug had been pulled out, everybody had left and it all went eerily quiet.

But not for long. **Ivy** continued:

> But soon after that, I remember seeing hundreds of soldiers, wounded in the fighting in northern France and many of them on stretchers, on the platforms of Southampton station waiting to be taken to hospital.

Another woman in the WRNS also described the scene on Southampton Docks soon after that:

> I saw hundreds of German prisoners of war and I suddenly became aware of the indescribable tragedy and horror of war. These were no proud and noble specimens of the Aryan race but a pathetic collection of underfed, tired and ill-looking youths wearing the ragged remains of uniforms. with a forlorn and hopeless look in their eyes.

Shades of British soldiers after Dunkirk, four years earlier?

Barbara Roy was also in the WRNS in 1944 but her job was controlling the movement of planes. She also remembered the excitement of D-Day very clearly:

The lead-up to D-Day was very tense. I was stationed at Lee-on-Solent, which is between Portsmouth and Southampton. There had already been one false alarm when it was cancelled at the last minute. My future husband was in the army and he was on an MTB [Motor Torpedo Boat] in the harbour waiting to go.

Then on D-Day I was terribly busy, sending fighters over to France. It was so exciting!

Eve Cherry was in the ATS and working as a driver for a blood transfusion team in Cornwall – the Bleeding Team, they called themselves:

We all knew that D-Day was coming – Churchill and Eisenhower had spoken about it on the wireless many times – and we kept seeing Americans all over southern England. They were a noisy lot! But of course, we didn't know when exactly it was going to be.

I stumbled on D-Day by accident. Very early on 6 June 1944, I had to drive a lorry with supplies of blankets from Truro across Bodmin Moor to a US Army camp on the other side of the moor. It was a beautiful summer's day, I remember, and I arrived at the American camp, which I'd visited many times before. But this time it was completely deserted, like a ghost town.

It was eerie. Tables were askew, chairs were pushed back, half-eaten food was still on the plates and the coffee wasn't yet cold. But there was absolutely no one around apart from a solitary caretaker. D-Day had finally arrived and all those soldiers had left in the night and were now fighting or being killed on the beaches of Normandy.

VE DAY

Over the next eleven months there was a lot more fighting as the Allied armies advanced westwards through northern France and then into Germany. Finally, on 8 May 1945, came VE (Victory in Europe) Day, when Allied forces finally and officially announced the unconditional surrender of Germany in Europe.

Previous to that, on 25 April, Allied and Soviet forces had met at the River Elbe. In a symbolic photo, 2nd Lieutenant William Robertson (US Army) and Lieutenant Alexander Silvashko (Red Army) stood facing each other with hands clasped and arms round each other's shoulders. The German Army was effectively destroyed and the war in Europe was, to all intents and purposes, over.

Five days later, holed up in his *Führerbunker* in Berlin, Hitler poisoned himself, his Alsatian dog, Blondi, and his wife of one day, Eva Braun, with cyanide capsules. For good measure, he then shot himself in the right temple with his Walther PP pistol. In accordance with his prior instructions, their remains were carried up the stairs, doused in petrol and set alight in the Reich Chancellery garden.

General Alfred Jodl, representing the German High Command, travelled to Eisenhower's headquarters in Rheims to seek terms for an end to the war. At 2.41 a.m. on Monday, 7 May, he signed the unconditional surrender of German forces, to take effect at 11.01 p.m., the next day.

In London, 8 May dawned grey and with a light drizzle. But as soon as the news got out the mood was transformed. At 3 p.m., Churchill broadcast to the nation and his official car was pushed, rather than driven, from 10 Downing Street along Whitehall to the House of Commons by a cheering crowd of exultant, joyful people.

A massive hokey-cokey snaked round and round Queen Victoria's statue in front of Buckingham Palace. The huge crowds, amounting to over a million, shouted, again and again, 'We want the King, we want the King!' The king and his family did not disappoint them. When the royal family, together with the Prime Minister came onto the balcony of the palace, the cheers were deafening and went on and on and on. For a short time, the two daughters of the king and queen, Elizabeth and Margaret, managed to sneak out of a back door of the palace and wander incognito among the crowds.

Meanwhile, all over the country, buildings were floodlit, ships hooted, searchlights cut giant Vs in the sky, bonfires were lit, church bells pealed, bunting was unfurled and fireworks exploded. People everywhere linked arms, climbed lamp-posts, jumped into fountains and crammed themselves into and on top of cars, lorries and buses. The war was, for the most part, finally over. Most people were exhausted but they still summoned up the energy to sing, dance, hug, kiss and be merry.

Churchill's victory speech that day was greeted ecstatically and the crowds cheered long and loud – he, more than anyone else, had the ability to articulate what the whole nation felt. That night, street lights were switched back on all over Britain and children who'd never known anything like it thought it was some sort of fairyland.

Every woman I spoke to had clear memories of the day the war ended, in Europe at least. **Vera Bartlett**, who'd been through so many trials and tribulations looking after three small children while her husband Ted was away, felt perhaps more than anything an overwhelming sense of relief on VE Day. And she was determined to mark the occasion:

> On the day the end of the war was announced, I managed to persuade someone to look after the children while I went up to London with a girlfriend. We went where the crowd went, we didn't have much choice, and some people threw crackers and fireworks from balconies and upstairs windows. That was a bit alarming, I remember.
>
> Of course, everyone wanted to see the king and queen on the balcony at Buckingham Palace so, along with hundreds of thousands of other people, we made our way up the Mall, everyone singing and dancing, with fireworks going off everywhere. There wasn't much drunkenness, probably because beer was rationed.
>
> And then finally we made it to Buckingham Palace and when the royal family came out onto the balcony, there was a huge cheer and we all waved again and again and shouted for them to come out just one more time.

In fact, they came out eight times altogether.

Meanwhile, **Diana England**, working at Bletchley Park near Reading, had this to say:

> On the day the end of the war was announced, I shed a few tears – well, quite a lot of tears actually – for my brother Tony, who'd been killed in the war. It seemed such jolly rotten luck that he'd fought so bravely but not lived to be with me on this simply wonderful, happy day.
>
> Then I and some friends hitched a lift to London on an open lorry. There, in London, I made my way to the Mall. I can't really describe the scene there, it was a seething mass of people, all dancing and singing and so very happy. My friend Isa and I went to Downing Street hoping to see Churchill, but of course he was at the palace with the royal family.
>
> I remember lots of servicemen climbed onto the tops of statues and up drainpipes and lamp-posts and then waved to the crowds below and the

crowds kept shouting up at them, 'Higher! Go on, higher!' I remember a sailor got to the very top of a very tall lamp-post and conducted the crowd with a beer bottle as we all sang 'There'll Always be an England'.

How we ever got home I don't know, but somehow we did!

Barbara Roy was a Wren with a great sense of fun and she certainly took the opportunity to celebrate. She was stationed on the south coast at Lee-on-Solent but, like **Vera** and **Diana**, she found the time to travel up to London for the celebrations:

On VE Day, what a party! I went to a nightclub in London called Club 400 and I didn't get home till 2 a.m. And then I had to be up at 6.30 a.m.! I felt dead! Everyone was quite mad.

This sense of elation and sheer joy was almost universal. **Margaret Walton** was typical:

I'll never forget the day the war ended. I was running to catch the bus to work when a friend shouted out to me, 'Where are you going?' so I told her and she said, 'Haven't you heard? The war has ended!' So I threw my handbag up into the air and went to the pub and I think I spent all day there, celebrating, singing and laughing. My parents came to join us and together we had such a bloody marvellous day.

Joan Watkins' memories of the end of the war were similar in some ways:

I was working at Southmead Hospital when somebody ran up and told me that the war had ended and then asked me if I'd like to go up to the Downs that evening to celebrate, but I was on my way there with a couple of friends when a small car full of young RAF officers stopped and told us that there wasn't a party there after all and we'd be much better off with them. So I sat on one of the airmen's knees in that very full car and then we had a party back in their RAF quarters. As far as I can remember, we danced all evening and most of the night celebrating the end of the war. It had been a long time coming.

Brenda Gimson, living in Hampshire while her husband was still away in Scotland with the Fleet Air Arm, remembered this about VE Day:

We walked through the village after dark and every house and cottage had switched every light on and opened every curtain, and the church bells rang out. But it wasn't a warning that the Germans were invading. It was to celebrate the end of the war. It was a thrilling and emotional moment for us all which I'll never forget.

Ruby Spragg, who'd worked so hard for most of the war at Bristol's Central Station, certainly deserved to celebrate the end of the war:

I'll never forget the day the war ended. People were running up and down the street, shouting and dancing. At first, I wondered what all the fuss was about but then my mother told me. She was crying, really sobbing, with joy.

And then there were street parties and everyone entered into the spirit of it. Our neighbour Don brought his piano out into the street and he played it for hours while everyone joined in all the songs. We didn't get any sleep. The parties went on and on because we all had the day off work the next day. It was a magnificent and happy end to the war which I'll never forget.

Ruby then added a sobering postscript, 'A man called Boswell climbed the tower of the local church to ring the bells to celebrate and the poor man fell and broke his back – silly bugger!'

Margaret Bowring lived near **Ruby Spragg** in central Bristol and she also remembered the parties and celebrations:

My father got together some old rusty saucepan lids and as we danced and sang we banged them together in time with the music. What a noise!

Dad had somehow managed to keep a bottle of whisky for this special day and when friends and neighbours came into our shop we drained it in no time, drinking from cups because we didn't have enough glasses. Then, when there was no more whisky left, we ended up banging on the shop counter with anything we could find and singing 'Whistle while you work, Hitler is a twerp, Mussolini bit his weenie, And now it doesn't squirt!'

Josephine Clements remembered that in her street they had a street party:

All the neighbours got together and donated food and I was amazed at the quantity and quality of what people gave, considering food rationing was so strict. Later, we lit a bonfire in the middle of the road but were shocked when the police arrived and told us to put it out – immediately.

'But why?' we asked.

'Because that fire's right on top of a gas main!'

So we did put it out, as fast as we could.

Lorna McNab had her own very personal account of the end of the war:

I'll never forget the day the war ended. I was 14, it was the evening and I was in a café with some friends at the top of Blackboy Hill. Somebody came dashing into the cafe and told us the news. 'The war's over!' People were already dancing in the street so we went out and linked arms and formed lines across the road and started dancing all the way down Whiteladies Road. I remember a car tried to get past us and someone tied a dustbin lid to its back bumper and then that dustbin lid made a terrible banging noise as it was dragged along the road.

Anyway, that dancing in the street was all quite spontaneous and hundreds of people came to join in, forming line after line behind us, singing and dancing all the way down Park Street. By the time we got to College Green, which was about 2 miles down the road, we were very, very tired and we just collapsed onto the grass. After that, we talked and sang and danced all night although I was only 14!

It was nearly dawn when I eventually got home. I was terrified of what my parents were going to say, especially my father, who had quite a temper. I sat on the front doorstep for a long time wondering what to do. But then I heard the sound of my mother in the kitchen lighting the kettle so I called to her very quietly. I'll never forget the look of relief on her face when she saw me, home and safe. And that was the end of the war for me.

Rosemary Strydom had a similar story to tell, except that she was in a very different place – Rome, 'I'll never forget the parties, the shouting, the singing, the dancing, most of it in the streets. The Italians who, after all, had been our enemies until quite recently, seemed as happy as we all were!'

Of the two diarists who have figured so prominently in this book, **HJF** wrote on 8 May:

VE Day! Mr Churchill broadcast 'Ceasefire' at 3 this afternoon. Thank God! Thank God! But how few bells can ring from their church towers in Bristol today! We are a sad city of ruins. The young lads want to celebrate with noise so they have taken the lids off the pig bins, clashing them together like cymbals as they pass our house on the way to the city centre. I stand on the verandah tonight and look towards Bath: I can see red glows and I am so grateful they are not the result of a blitz. Bonfires are lit and from the centre comes the hum of a city rejoicing. My one regret is that somewhere in the distant East some fine young English and American boy may be dying or killed tonight.

In contrast, **Eleanor Frost** wrote on 7 May:

The unconditional surrender of the German forces by land, sea and air. Mother and I went to a Thanksgiving Service in Leigh Woods church. Afterwards I attended a fireworks party when an effigy of Hitler was burnt. Then two friends, unable to find food in the city, came here to supper and to hear the King's Broadcast to the Empire and the World at 9 p.m. At 10.30 p.m. Mother, Edith and I went to the Observatory where there was a bonfire. Cheering and singing came from the City. It is difficult to realise it is all over.

Two days later, on Wednesday, 9 May, she wrote:

Tonight Bristol was twinkling with lights and this made us realise the peace more than the night before when owing to people being out of doors perhaps there were not so many lights. It has all come so quickly during the last few days that it has a numbing effect. I feel still that [it] is almost dream-like!

Rose Jennings also remarked on this big change that the end of the war meant, 'The sheer joy of being able to walk the streets with all the lights on again. Apart from that, I think the overwhelming feeling was one of terrific relief.'

Dr Mary Jones also described the end of the war, 'The day I heard that the war had ended I was absolutely delighted. We were so desperately tired of the war, so relieved that it was finally all over.' And that just about summed up the feelings of most of the women I spoke to, sheer delight and an overwhelming feeling of tremendous relief.

Lorna Green was slightly less than enthusiastic about VE Day:

Finally, the end of the war in Europe. But it was confused and confusing for us. I can remember saying, 'But has the war really ended?' ... But there was no great sense of jubilation, as far as I was concerned. The war in the East continued, while we gradually learned of the full horror of concentration camps.

Eve Cherry also summarised the end of the war for her:

After D-Day I just carried on working with my 'bleeding team', doing what I always wanted to do – drive. But it was all a bit of an anti-climax really. And by the time I was eventually discharged, I was so very tired of the war – I think we all were.

And then one final comment, 'I didn't keep my uniform, apart from my skirt which I dyed navy blue. I wore that until it was completely worn out!'

VJ Day

And as if one celebration on VE Day wasn't enough, **Barbara Roy** also remembered another good excuse for another good party on 5 August. 'On VJ Day we had a party at lunchtime and then tennis in the afternoon and another party in the evening!'

Peggy Turner remembered the end of the war all too well because, for her at least, VE Day wasn't really a cause for much joy while her husband Keith was still away in Burma, fighting the Japanese:

But then finally came VJ Day. News of the end of the war came late in the evening and I was just getting ready for bed. But then I walked with a friend, and me in my nightie and a dressing gown, to Whiteladies Road where the revels were just starting. Then, lured by the increasing feeling of excitement, I walked down to Queens Road and then Park Street and then on into the city centre where things were really going on. And all this in my nightie and dressing gown!

To sum up her feelings and experiences during the war, **Diana England**, who had started out as an ACW2, the lowest rank in the WAAFs, had this to say:

Before the war, just after I'd left boarding school, my parents decided they were going to send me off to an awfully smart finishing school in Paris. But then the war came along and, do you know what, that 'finished' me instead! But looking back on it now, I'm so terribly glad it did!

So that was it then, for all the women I spoke to – the end of a long, destructive war. During the conflict about 3 per cent of the human race, up to 85 million people altogether, most of them civilians, had died. Britain had teetered on the edge of defeat.

But for all these women, it was an experience they would never forget. Their lives had been transformed and most of them had grown from girls into women. One of them had worked on a Woolworth's sweets counter but went on to milk a herd of cows, more or less single-handed; another had progressed from being a gauche, inexperienced medical student to being the doctor in charge of a prisoner-of-war camp housing a number of convinced Nazis; another had spent years as a single mother, like my own mother-in-law, wishing and desperately hoping that her husband would eventually return alive. And for another, it had been the time when her prowess at the table-tennis table led to meeting and falling in love with a young American who was to be the love of her life, only for him to be killed on D-Day.

For some, it had been a frightening, anxious and arduous time while others confessed to taking full advantage of the newfound freedoms which the war offered them, to the point where they admitted to having a wonderful, hugely enjoyable experience. They grew up fast, because they had to, and in the process discovered in themselves new qualities and abilities they hadn't even dreamed of. And all of them had, in their very different ways, demonstrated stoicism, resilience, courage and a tremendous zest for life.

My one regret, having finished writing this book, is that for the great majority of the many women that I interviewed its publication has come too late. Like almost all of their generation, they have since died. But at least their children, grandchildren and great-grandchildren will now know what these women did during the war. My mother-in-law, Mary Fox, to whom this book is dedicated, I hope would be happy to know that.

Bibliography

The primary sources for this book were the many women, more than sixty, in fact, whom I interviewed over eight years. They were mostly in their eighties, a few in their nineties and a couple were centenarians. They willingly and with enthusiasm answered my many questions, recounted their memories and recalled innumerable details.

I wrote their stories and visited them a second and sometimes a third time to make certain that what I had written was a true record of what they had told me.

I was kindly given permission to quote from the memoirs of two women, Audrey Swindells and Lorna Green, and the wartime diary of Joan Hancox. I have also quoted from the diaries of two other women. Eleanor Frost wrote copiously about events in her life throughout the war years. When she died, she left her diaries to the Bristol Records Office, who gave me permission to quote from them. I have also quoted extensively from a pseudonymous book entitled *Diary of a Bristol Woman*.

FURTHER READING

Adie, Kate, *Corsets to Camouflage* (Hodder and Stoughton, 2004).
Calder, Angus, *The People's War* (Pimlico, 1992).
Channel 4, *The 1940's House* (TV series and book, 2000).
Costello, John, *Love, Sex and War* (Collins, 1985).
Fisher, Lucy, *Women in the War* (Harper Collins, 2021).
Garfield, Simon, *We are at War* (Ebury Press, 2006).

Longmate, Norman, *How We Lived Then* (Pimlico, 2002).

Malcolmson, Patricia, and Robert, *Women at the Ready* (Little Brown, 2013).

Minns, Raynes, *Bombers and Mash* (Virago, 2012).

Nicholson, Virginia, *Millions Like Us* (Penguin, 2011).

Powell, Bob, and Nigel Westacott, *The Women's Land Army* (The History Press, 2009).

Reader's Digest, *Life on the Home Front* (Reader's Digest, 1994).

Sheridan, Dorothy, *Wartime Women* (Phoenix, 2009).

Stockwell, Andrew H. (ed.), *Diary of a Bristol Woman* (Bristol Central Library, reference section, 1948).